When Your Child Is Difficult

Solve Your Toughest Child-Raising Problems with a Four-Step Plan That Works

Mel Silberman, Ph.D.

Research Press
2612 North Mattis Avenue
Champaign, Illinois 61821

This book was originally published by Warner Books, Inc., under the title *Confident Parenting: Solve Your Toughest Child-Raising Problems with a Four-Step Plan That Works!*

Copies of this book may be ordered from the publisher at the address given on the title page.

Cover design by Loren Kirkwood
Composition by Tradewinds Imaging
Printed by United Graphics

ISBN 0–87822–361–4
Library of Congress Catalog Number 95–70413

To my mother, Elsie Silberman.
May her memory be for a blessing.

Contents

Acknowledgments

When Your Child Is Difficult has evolved from a fifteen-year journey of helping children in a wide variety of families, classrooms, and other settings. For much of that journey, Dr. Susan Wheelan has been my fellow traveler. The guiding principles and action plans found in this book come from the stimulating professional relationship I have enjoyed with Dr. Wheelan.

During these fifteen years, I have had the support of colleagues at Temple University for my explorations in parent education and family therapy. To all of you who have encouraged my work, I owe you thanks. I also owe a considerable debt to Salvador Minuchin. From my first days of training at the Philadelphia Child Guidance Clinic, my thinking about how to help parents and children has been profoundly shaped by Dr. Minuchin's ideas on family structure and change.

Professional colleagues in my home town of Princeton, New Jersey, have graciously reviewed the manuscript of this book, pointing out unclear passages and cheering my efforts. My thanks to Lewis Gantwerk, Psy.D., Elliott Gursky, M.D., and Maxine Farmer, M.S.W.

A special note of appreciation goes to my wife Shoshana for her steadfast encouragement of my work with parents and children and her years of love, devotion, and affirmation. Our children Steven, Lisa, and Gabe are lucky she is their mother. And I am lucky to be their father.

Introduction

This book has one overriding goal: to give parents (and all other child-care providers) the confidence to help children change their behavior when they are being difficult.

When are children difficult? The possibilities are, of course, endless. Many children are difficult during a particular developmental phase: perhaps colicky as an infant, headstrong as a toddler, argumentative in the elementary school years, or moody as an adolescent. The specific difficulties they pose can be far-ranging, such as resistance to toilet training, fear of new people, poor sleeping habits, watching too much TV, failure to make friends, sloppiness and disorganization, violent rages, underachievement, and substance abuse.

Some children have behavioral difficulties stemming from chronic conditions, including physical handicaps, developmental disabilities, chronic illnesses, learning differences, and even constitutional shyness. Other children may be experiencing problems adjusting to particular events such as a divorce or a move to a new community. *All children can be difficult as they are learning to grow up and behave maturely.*

Regardless of the category your child may fit, this book is intended for you. It will teach you the ten choices you have to help your child. As you will learn, these ten choices apply regardless of your child's age, the severity of the behavior, or the cause.

Furthermore, this book will help you in another way. All the thousands of parents I have counseled feel confused, fearful, and even angry at times. They ask themselves: Should I be lenient or strict? Have my actions been damaging? Why is my child like this? The trouble with being confused, fearful, or angry is that children are denied the confident direction they need from us.

Children require parents who have a surer grasp of what to do rather than parents who fret and worry about what might happen or explode after it does. This book will give you that confidence.

Of course, confidence is not something that can be obtained in one or two magic moves. Moreover, once we've got a little bit of it, children are adept at eroding whatever modest gains we've made. To make matters worse, we parents today often have limited time and energy. With these factors in mind, *When Your Child Is Difficult* is a short book that gives busy, tired, and confidence-shaken parents realistic advice. *When Your Child Is Difficult* —

- Contains a simple, four-step plan that is easy to remember and put into practice.

- Gives you guidelines you can use over and over again as your children grow and develop. It's also a reference you'll never find out-of-date or trendy.

- Empowers parents. You will feel supported, not admonished. You will believe in yourself—and your children will be the beneficiaries.

- Has been successfully field tested with a wide range of parents—from every socioeconomic, racial, and ethnic background; parents with small tots and parents with towering teens; parents of average kids and parents of children with very special needs.

You, too, can join the thousands of parents who have found the ideas in *When Your Child Is Difficult* to make a big difference to their family.

PART ONE

The Building Blocks

1

The Dual Role of Parents

All children can be difficult. For some the difficulties are short-lived, for others the difficulties are persistent.

Whether your child is strong-willed, shy, fearful, slow, or simply immature at times, his behavior can change. It isn't easy and there are no simple formulas, but this book will give you some helpful guidance.

The best way to start learning how to help your difficult child is to complete a little exercise. On the next page is a fill-in-the-blanks activity I call *My Child's Needs*. It takes only three minutes of your time and it could represent one of the most important three minutes you've spent with yourself in a while.

My Child's Needs

Fill in as many blanks as possible during the next three minutes. Go as fast as you can. Ignore the columns marked E and C. If you have more than one child who concerns you, choose the one who is the greatest concern because the exercise can only be done once. If you are co-parenting your children, it may be especially valuable for the other parent to complete this exercise on a separate sheet of paper and compare responses.

Fill in the blanks

E   C

_____ My child needs _____ from me _____ .

_____ My child needs _____ from me _____ .

_____ My child needs _____ from me _____ .

_____ My child needs _____ from me _____ .

_____ My child needs _____ from me _____ .

_____ My child needs _____ from me _____ .

_____ My child needs _____ from me _____ .

_____ My child needs _____ from me _____ .

_____ My child needs _____ from me _____ .

_____ My child needs _____ from me _____ .

GIVING CHILDREN LOVE WITHOUT STRINGS ATTACHED

Before asking you to evaluate your responses to *My Child's Needs*, I'd like you to consider the plight of Billy, a little guy who wields more power than is good for him.

> Billy, age three, had refused to go to sleep at night by himself as long as his parents could remember. One of them always had to stay in the room until he fell asleep. Although Billy's parents were annoyed by this arrangement, they viewed Billy's request as an extraordinary need for attention and parental comfort. To soothe Billy, they decided to make an especially big fuss over bedtime rituals and caresses, and then try to tiptoe out of the room when he seemed drowsy. Every time, however, Billy caught them in the act and protested with sobs and tears. They wondered . . . since we are being so reasonable, why isn't Billy? Resentment toward Billy increased, but so did their guilt over having such negative feelings toward their son. Thus they tried anew to give Billy the additional time and love he demanded, but the result was always the same.

Although well-meaning, Billy's parents have confused two related but different parts of being a parent—caring and guiding. Billy needs lots of care, but he also *needs* parents who quietly and firmly insist that he go to sleep by himself. Learning to do this will do his self-worth more good than extra hugs.

Over the past fifteen years, I have spoken to more than ten thousand parents. Each time I address a new group, I begin by posing the same question I just asked you: *What do you think your child needs from you?*

As well it should be, *love* is the first response heard from the audience. Then other words flow such as *attention, understanding, patience, acceptance,* and *time.* Only with prompting do the responses begin to change to words like guidance, discipline, values, direction, or rules.

The pattern is quite predictable. Responses that refer to the "caring job" of parents usually head the list. Responses that refer to the "executive job" of parents usually lag behind.

The *caring role* of parents includes all those acts that directly let a child know that she is accepted, nurtured, supported, and loved. By contrast the *executive role* of parents includes all those acts that directly let a child know that he is under the influence and direction of an adult who is in charge of the child's well-being.

The caring role is our way of accommodating a child's limitations. She may have problems feeling secure, understood, and capable. When we are loving, attentive, understanding, patient, etc., we provide the basic protection needed to face life.

In the caring mode, a child is accepted where she currently is. *Change is not expected.* Other benefits can be derived from carrying out our caring role.

1. **Trust:** Children form basic feelings of trust in others from the experience of being responded to and supported by their parents. Without this basic trust, children never learn to trust themselves.

2. **Reinforcement:** The degree to which parents have the power to reinforce (or discourage) their children's behavior depends upon whether children feel that they are valued. When children feel continually rejected, they become immune to parental rewards (and punishments).

3. **Support:** Children cannot weather the frustration caused by their own limitations and failures without parental support. Continual frustration causes children to give up and not care.

4. **Giving:** In order for children to have emotional nourishment to give to others when they become older, they must receive emotional nourishment when they are young.

The executive role has a very different emphasis. Here, *we are motivators of change.* In the executive mode, we are encouraging children (through discipline, responsibilities, guidance, choices, etc.) to "get their act together"—to become more mature, to grow and develop.

Children reap important benefits by our willingness to carry out our executive role.

1. **Reassurance:** Children are reassured by having parents who make decisions about the directions their lives are taking and the rules by which they must live. I grant that when children

continually protest parental decisions, they do not seem reassured. But, actually, the best way for these children to really find out if their parents are confident (and reassuring) decision-makers is to see if they don't buckle when they are tested.

2. **Practice:** Children obtain valuable practice early in life when we say no and when we confront them with demands for responsible behavior. When children do not get this "practice," they grow to be either overly demanding or excessively afraid of displeasing others.

3. **Appreciation:** Children are appreciated more when their parents help them act responsibly. If we don't do everything in our power to help change our children's behavior, they wind up the losers. Instead of receiving approval from other children and adults, they are resented and even rejected.

4. **Self-reliance:** Children become more self-reliant when more is expected of them. When parents focus their executive energies around expectations that push children to take care of themselves, children don't become dependent on having things done for them.

Children need parents who are comfortable both in their caring and executive roles. Indeed, it could be argued that security to children, particularly when they are difficult, is represented by the presence of two seemingly opposite conditions: (1) their parents care for them dearly; and (2) their parents are willing to guide them even when their guidance is unpopular.

My question to parents, "What do you think your child needs from you?" taps inner beliefs about their priorities, beliefs that may be unconscious. I see no problem when parents lend considerable importance to their caring job. But if their inner beliefs indicate little room for the executive job, there is a big problem. Children may not only be deprived of the direction that more mature, more knowledgeable adults can provide, but also discover that their parents' love has "strings attached." Let me explain why.

Conflict between parents and children is inevitable. The two parties have different perspectives on almost everything: bedtimes, school achievement, TV, neatness, etc. A major reason for these varying perspectives is that children are not able to understand the world in the same way as adults. As children grow, so does their ability to understand events in more complex ways. During childhood, however, thought is quite self-centered and children tend to act impulsively on their wishes. As they mature, their self-centeredness and impulsiveness decrease. This is a long process, though, extending into adolescence.

What all this means is that parents must place limits on behavior even though the child cannot fully understand why. They must also teach values even though the child does not appreciate them. It does not matter if the parents in question have a permissive or strict approach to child rearing. Sooner or later, a parent has an executive job to perform.

When parents hold too dearly to the belief that their children need love, patience, understanding, and the like, they tend to use these caring behaviors to get their executive job done. The process is all too common: *Parents act nice in order to get their children to act nice in return*. I'll grant your wishes if you grant mine becomes the basis of parent-child relationships. Such an arrangement is usually not explicit. Instead, parents may think that they have a kind of implicit contract with their child that parental decency will be rewarded by child decency.

This caring with strings attached has one of two results. The child may comply with parental wishes in order to preserve parental love and approval, or the child may act to frustrate this implicit contract and cause parents to switch to intimidation tactics or heavy guilt trips. Either way, the child loses. Another case example may serve as further explanation.

> Jodie, age thirteen, was apathetic about school. Although
> of superior intelligence, she rarely put forth any effort
> unless what was being studied really interested her.
> Her mother, divorced for one year, interpreted Jodie's
> underachievement as a protest against her for leaving
> Jodie's father. On several occasions she tried to explain
> to Jodie why the divorce was necessary, but Jodie
> claimed she wasn't interested. Rebuffed in her attempt
> to communicate, the mother felt that the best thing to
> do was to give Jodie as much time as she could, going
> places, talking over dinner, and the like. These gestures,
> however, did not bring Jodie any closer and her schoolwork

began to deteriorate as well. Feeling totally unappreciated at this point, the mother found herself complaining a lot to Jodie about how hard it had been to manage since her father had left and, in return, how hard Jodie had been to live with. These remarks, of course, did little to change the situation. Eventually, Jodie's mother was helped to see that Jodie wanted a strong, confident parent, not a guilt-ridden mother. The mother set up clear rules about homework and arranged with Jodie's teachers to give weekly feedback on her school performance. Jodie's mother also kept open the lines of communication with her daughter but didn't press Jodie about her feelings until she was ready to share them. Eventually, Jodie did.

This love without strings attached attitude is the basis of a confident approach to parenting. Confident parenting is a deep concern for the well-being of children communicated in a straight-forward, enthusiastic way. It is also an expression of commitment rather than a tool for manipulation. Because parents who care also act in charge, they don't confuse caring with guiding. Maybe the willingness to guide children is itself one of the most important acts that caring parents can perform.

Confident parents give their children lots of hugs and encouragement, but they also know that, ultimately, children need parents who are their leaders, not their followers, parents who act rather than react, and parents who assume authority instead of abdicating it.

The activity on the next page will help you interpret your beliefs about your children's needs.

Interpreting Your Beliefs About Children's Needs

The focus now is not on Billy's or Jodie's parents, but on you. *Is your view of what your child needs from you very one-sided? How comfortable are you with both the executive and caring roles?*

1. Go back to page 4 and look over your responses to the question, "What does my child need from me?"

2. Place a check in the E column next to responses that are used to perform your executive job (see the list below).

3. Place a check in the C column next to responses that are used to perform your caring job (see the list below).

4. Sometimes responses do not easily fit either category. If you are unsure how to categorize a response, leave it blank.

5. If more of your responses are categorized E or categorized C, your view of your child's needs may be too one-sided. How balanced a list are they?

E Responses	C Responses
Advice	Acceptance
Choices	Attention
Coaching	Communication
Consistency	Encouragement
Direction	Food/money/clothes
Discipline	Friendship
Education	Help
Guidance	Love
Limits	Patience
Religion	Protection
Responsibility	Respect
Structure	Time
Supervision	Trust
Values	Understanding

BEING IN CHARGE AND INVOLVED

Raising children requires a strong commitment both to the executive and caring roles and the needs each role fulfills. You can be a positive influence on your children's development if you are willing and able to be IN CHARGE and INVOLVED.

An *in charge* parent:

- Can say no firmly when children want something that is unreasonable or unhealthy for them or others.

- Can convey clear, positive expectations that children act responsibly.

- Can provide choices when, in the parent's best judgment, the children will not be harmed.

An *involved* parent:

- Can make time for children and show interest in them.

- Can support and encourage children even when they are having trouble.

- Can listen to children's feelings and share his own.

When children are difficult, parents often have a hard time believing that they can be both in charge and involved. Instead, they feel the need to choose between the two. Some parents, for example, are afraid to take charge because they fear the loss of their child's love. Other parents are concerned that their child will lose respect and take advantage of them if they act too friendly.

It is *not* necessary to choose between the executive and caring roles. This book will show you several ways in which the roles can be blended. While there are times when you need to emphasize either executive actions or caring actions in order to resolve a specific problem, generally speaking, both expressions of parenting can exist side by side.

Another difficulty I have observed for parents with difficult children is avoiding extremes in carrying out each role. You can *overdo* or *underplay* being in charge. You can do the same when being involved. The possibilities are best described in the following diagram.

Confusing ◄─────── In charge ───────► Rigid

Distant ◄─────── Involved ───────► Entangled

Let us explore each of these sets of extremes.

Confusing ◄─── In Charge ───► Rigid

Confusing parents are inconsistent and unclear. Children may know that such parents are displeased sometimes by their behavior, but they never know for sure how insistent their parents are that the behavior changes. Children may also know that their parents expect certain rules to be followed, but often it's not clear exactly what those rules are.

> Take, for example, Bette and Joe. Their son Chris had cerebral palsy and needed considerable assistance getting ready for school. Nonetheless, he was capable of performing some of the tasks involved in getting dressed, toileting, toothbrushing, etc. For years Bette and Joe had been upset at Chris's dawdling in the morning. Although they usually berated Chris for his lack of "cooperation," they almost always caved in and gave Chris the assistance he did not require. Bette and Joe would have been less confusing if they had identified exactly what Chris's job was and what was theirs, and consistently expected Chris to do his share.

In contrast to confusing parents, *rigid* parents are controlling and inflexible. Although they may be well-meaning, rigid parents don't allow children to make some decisions themselves or attempt to control their own behavior. They may also stubbornly cling to their positions even if workable compromises are possible.

> Jessica, for instance, was a ten-year-old child with mild learning disabilities. Besides attending a special school that provided individualized instruction tailored to her needs, Jessica, at her parents' insistence, went to a learning therapist twice weekly. Jessica felt under pressure and estranged from peers by this arrangement, but her parents didn't give her any direct say in the matter. As a result,

Jessica developed physical symptoms, such as stomach-aches, as an indirect way of protesting.

Distant ◄——— Involved ———► Entangled

In the realm of parental involvement, there are equally conflicting possibilities. As we saw in the diagram on page 12, overinvolvement can lead to entanglement.

Entangled parents are overprotective and intrusive. They feel every frustration and distress children experience and rarely allow children to get over a tough hurdle by themselves. Many parents fall into this trap. They expect a closeness with their child that the child finds overwhelming and often suffocating.

> Adele was a single parent with a teenage daughter, Julie. The two fought like sisters over several matters. For example, Adele read her daughter's diary and listened to her phone calls, and Julie was rude to Adele's friends. They looked, talked, and thought alike. Ever since Adele's divorce from Julie's father, Adele had hovered over Julie, encouraging a close relationship and identifying with her moods. When Julie became an adolescent, she started to rebel and Adele overreacted. The two were now entangled in conflict.

Distant parents, by comparison, are aloof and self-preoccupied. They frequently tune out when children are talking and spend little time with them. Such parents are less likely to initiate words of support or encouragement, absorbed instead in their own thoughts. Such parents are not necessarily cold, uncaring people.

> Jon and Bonnie, for example, were both busy with successful careers. Try as they might to have quality time with their two boys, ages five and three, they were simply too tired and stressed. They also allowed business-related phone calls to intrude upon family time in the evening. Naturally, the boys, somewhat difficult to begin with, became severe behavior problems as a way to receive the attention they lacked. This further stressed Jon and Bonnie and distanced them from the boys.

You should not conclude that certain extremes go together automatically. Rigid parents are often distant, but others are entangled. Additionally, confusing parents can be either entangled or distant. Thus, there are four extreme types:

1. Rigid—Entangled

2. Rigid—Distant

3. Confusing—Entangled

4. Confusing—Distant*

It is unlikely that any of us fits these types all the time. All parents vary in their behavior, but many lean in a particular direction.

Consider your relationship with each of your children, particularly the one who is most difficult. Does it fit any of the four types listed above?

WHAT YOU CAN DO TO CHANGE THE RELATIONSHIP

It isn't easy to remain *in charge* and avoid the extremes of being *unclear* or *rigid*. Nor is it easy to remain *involved* rather than *distant* or *entangled*. At times you are under stress from the difficulties your child poses and cannot direct your own behavior at will. So treat the words *in charge* and *involved* as goals worth striving for but not always attainable.

Here are some suggestions to alter your relationship.

To be less *rigid*:

- Identify a small first step your child can take instead of seeking a major change in behavior.

- Give up seeking some behavior changes and concentrate on others.

- Provide limited choices for your child ("you may clean your room anytime until 9:00 tonight").

---

*These types are derived from David Olson's model of family functioning.

To be less *confusing*:

- Don't make threats or promises you won't back up.
- When you make a request, make it clear whether it is a wish or a demand.
- Identify the specific behavior you want from your child (more about this in Chapter 3).

To be less *entangled*:

- Allow your child to have some likes and dislikes different from your own.
- Find other outlets in your life besides your most difficult child (a great place to begin is focusing on your other children, your spouse, or something you'd like to learn).
- Be available to hear your child's concerns, but don't assume total responsibility for solving them.

To be less *distant*:

- Give support to your child to help him get over a really tough hurdle.
- Share an activity you rarely or never have experienced with your child.
- Listen more than you talk to your child.

Something else you can do is to think about the needs *you* have as a parent. One way to do this involves another fill-in-the-blanks activity (on the next page) that is the direct opposite of the first one you did. I call it *My Wishes As a Parent.*

My Wishes As a Parent

Fill in as many blanks as possible during the next three minutes. Go as fast as you can and be honest! If you have more than one child, choose the one who is the greatest concern. Ask your co-parent to do the activity on a separate sheet and compare responses.

Fill in the blanks

I want _____ from my child.

I want _____ from my child.

I want _____ from my child.

I want _____ from my child.

I want _____ from my child.

1. Look over your responses. Most of them are perfectly appropriate things to want from your child. When our wishes are overly strong, however, we may be asking for trouble. For example, when we are too dependent on *love* or *acceptance* from our children, we might try too hard to please them or be popular with them. When we are too dependent on *peace* and *quiet* from our children, we might avoid them too much instead of giving them adequate attention. An extreme desire for *obedience* from children can lead us to be controlling and harsh. Positive accomplishments that bring us *enjoyment* and *pride* from our children are certainly desirable, but coveting them too much can tend to make us overinvolved in our children's successes and failures.

2. Place a check next to any wishes on your list that might get you "in trouble" as a parent. The more you are aware of these troublemaking needs, the easier it will be for you to hold them in check so that they don't interfere with the goals of being in charge and involved.

One particularly troublesome wish deserves special attention—the wish for REASSURANCE. You must be very careful not to desire too much reassurance *from your child*, even though your child needs reassurance *from you*.

When parents are anxious about a child, they often look to the child's moods and reactions for guidance on what to do and as a gauge for how they are doing. (Have you ever said to yourself, "I'm not very popular with my kid today.") However, your child's response to you may be a very poor guide as to how well you are doing. Let me explain why.

It takes time for a child to become accepting, let alone happy about any parental behavior she may not immediately like. Just remember the time you introduced your child as an infant to strained vegetables (or any other baby food not well received). To abandon what we think is right because a child thinks it is wrong can be a big mistake. Anyone with teenagers knows how true this is.

I'm not saying that we should ignore a child's feelings. Children should be heard, not just seen, but listening to children is not the same as being reassured by them. The better source of reassurance is *from other adults* who are close to you and close to your child (see Chapter 6).

Questions and Answers

When parents are introduced to the ideas in this chapter, they respond with enthusiasm and agreement. Nonetheless, parents raise some questions in order to understand their dual role better. Here are the most frequent questions I get.

1. *Don't we control young children too much by being "executives"?*

No. Being an "executive" doesn't mean that we should control everything in young children's lives, but it does mean that we are in the driver's seat calling the shots. We should decide what powers, decisions, and choices to give them. Gradually giving children a part in making their own decisions helps them develop a sense of their own competence. They also learn to live with the consequences of making up their own minds.

2. *Does the age of my child affect how much I am in charge and involved?*

Absolutely. As children get older, they need more freedom and require less care, but children never outgrow their need for strong, confident, in-charge parents who also stay involved in their lives. Many parents tend to overestimate how well teenagers, in particular, can do without parental caring and guidance.

3. *Should one parent be mainly "in charge" in the family?*

No. In a two-parent family, both parents need to be executives and both need to provide caring. When parents specialize in one of the two roles, it teaches children that both parents don't have to be minded and that both parents can't provide nurturing and support.

4. *Doesn't the executive job conflict with the caring job, especially for single parents?*

Many single parents feel that the caring job interferes with the executive job. This feeling comes from worrying too much that they will "lose" their children if they are firm. As we saw in the case of Jodie, children in single-parent families want to know that their parent is "in charge." Often, the best way for them to find out is to test the limits and give the parent a difficult time. Be reassured that they want to find out their parent is in charge.

5. *I hate to be a cop with my children. Do I have to be in charge all the time?*

Of course not. So long as you have established with your children that you make and enforce decisions on their behalf, you can forget about who's in charge and enjoy your children. Knowing that you are in charge is a lot different than always "acting" in charge.

6. *Is it too late if you've let your children take advantage of you for many years and have not established that you are in charge?*

It's never too late, but there is no better time than now to start. The best way to begin changing things is to pick out *one* area in which you would like to be more in charge.

Don't pick the most difficult challenge. Make up your mind that your children will listen to you at least in this one area (e.g., doing chores). Stay as calm as you can and persist in your efforts until things are better. Then go to another area, slowly building your authority.

2

Your Child Can Change

Of all the statements I make to parents, this one is the hardest to swallow: "Your child is capable of changing his behavior." It's not that parents don't wish this were true, but because of the continual frustrations many have had, it has often been easier to accept the difficulties and live with them as something over which one has no control.

Grace and George had a five-year-old son, Peter. Peter had a short attention span and boundless energy. Grace and George often joked that when Peter was born, he practically crawled off the delivery table! As a young child, he slept little, cried a lot, had several accidents, and, in short, was more difficult to handle than their three other children put together. Grace and George were considerably discouraged parents who had given up hope that Peter would ever calm down. At the same time, they were reluctant to use the medications for hyperactivity suggested to them. Having heard that hyperactivity decreases as a child gets older, they decided "to wait it out."

Fortunately, Grace and George's resignation was challenged by Peter's kindergarten teacher. She noticed that Peter did much better if he was given specific directions, consistent reinforcements, and a quiet, nondistracting environment in which to work and play. With the further help of a therapist, a program was designed to create similar conditions at home and to literally teach Peter how to attend to something longer. Within four weeks, there was a noticeable change in Peter's attention span and behavior control.

Sometimes parents are not aware they have been treating their child as if he was unable to change his behavior. They perceive themselves as parents who are making a conscientious effort to get their child to change, but the way they are communicating with their child conveys the idea that "we don't think you can do it."

Since October of his senior year in high school, Carl and his family were seeing a family therapist because Carl was depressed. In a therapy session late in December, Carl's parents raised their displeasure that Carl had not completed any of his college applications, even though they had been after him for weeks about his procrastination. The therapist invited Carl's parents to discuss the matter with Carl during the session. As the parents talked, the therapist observed that they were communicating with Carl as if he were a little child who needed repetition and a sweet tone of voice to grasp what was being said. The therapist was able to link Carl's depression and procrastination to the idea that he was treated like a child who was also expected to do grown-up things.

REMEMBER *MY FAIR LADY*?

In addition to being an entertaining musical show, *My Fair Lady* taught a powerful lesson in human relations. How we treat a person communicates our expectations or predictions about how that person will behave. People to whom we communicate negative expectations tend to respond negatively; people for whom we have positive expectations tend to respond positively. As Liza Doolittle puts it, "I shall always be a flower girl to Professor Higgins, because he always treats me as a flower girl, and always will, but I know I can be a lady to you, because you always treat me as a lady, and always will."

You can improve the chances of change in your child by being a purveyor of positive expectations. Actively communicating positive expectations is an effective antidote for both an attitude of complacency and an attitude of chronic dissatisfaction toward your child. You're letting your child know, without nagging, that you believe in his potential even if your child's present behavior isn't constructive.

Here are some suggestions for communicating positive expectations:

1. Don't condone unacceptable behavior that you know your child can correct. Otherwise your child will infer that you believe the behavior cannot change.

2. Avoid baby talk. Talk to your children at a level that is more mature than the one they presently use. Say what you want to once rather than incessantly repeating yourself. Let your child know that you believe she can get something done without your hovering over her or doing it yourself.

3. When your child is unsuccessful in accomplishing something, tell him, "Maybe you can't do this today, but I bet you can do it soon." Don't quit on your child.

IF I ONLY KNEW THE CAUSE

One of the common reasons parents give for expecting little or no change from their child is expressed in these words: "I really can't understand why my child is like this. If I only knew the cause."

I sympathize with this feeling. If a cause for a behavior can be found, a parent would have a better chance at fixing the problem. I urge you to take reasonable measures to discover hidden factors that account for the difficulties your child poses. For example, by all means have your child's hearing or vision checked if you suspect there are problems. I know of several children whose dislike of and even phobic reactions to school could be traced to such difficulties. If your child has experienced an emotional trauma or significant change recently, you should also seek help in understanding how it may be linked to current behaviors.

The problem with looking for causes, however, is that they are often hard to find. Moreover, even if a problem had a cause, it may persist for entirely different reasons. For example, your child may have been withdrawn in the company of other children because of shyness. But, her continued isolation may now be due to your overprotectiveness. Finally, some problems with children have no causes in the conventional sense, but are a result of processes in the family as a whole. Anorexia is a good example. In order to understand what has happened it would be necessary to untangle a complex of knots and threads. Even if this were possible, a simple remedy could not be easily found.

One of the best ways to understand a problem is to act on it in new ways and see what happens. I am not suggesting dangerous experiments, but I do believe that parents should not be paralyzed by their uncertainty about the causes of their child's behavioral difficulties. Don't be afraid of trying some brand-new approaches before you can establish (if ever) the reasons for your child's actions. (In Chapter 5, I discuss some new techniques you might utilize.)

Although some parents excuse children from change because they don't know the cause, other parents sometimes do the opposite: they blame a child's difficulties on false causes within the child. It began with: "She must be teething." Next was: "She's now in the terrible two's." On and on the child is viewed as someone controlled by forces outside a parent's influence, sometimes even "monsterish" ones. Salvador Minuchin, the renowned family therapist, quips:

> In families with young children, one of the most common problems to appear in a child guidance clinic is the preschooler described by parents as a "monster" who will not obey any rules. When a fifty-pound tyrant terrorizes an entire family, it must be assumed that she has an accomplice. For a three-foot tyrant to be taller than the rest of the family members, she has to be standing on the shoulders of one of the adults.*

Rather than view the child as hopelessly difficult, Minuchin finds the real "cause" in the way the parents are battling each

---

*Minuchin, S., and Fishman, H. C. *Family Therapy Techniques*, Cambridge, MA: Harvard University Press, 1981, p. 58.

other around the child. This diagnosis can lead to a change in the situation. Blaming matters on monsters, on teething, and on the terrible two's is the same as saying "boys will be boys," "that's adolescence for you," or "she's a middle child." Whenever we exaggerate or exonerate our child's problems, we stand in the way of change.

SOME BASIC REASONS THAT CHILDREN ARE DIFFICULT

Looking for specific causes behind your child's behavior may not be possible or fruitful, but it does make sense to have a general theory. The value of general theories is twofold:

1. They suggest an action direction.

2. They can be tested to see if they are valid.

Below are some of the basic reasons that children are difficult. Suggested actions are also given (see highlighted words). Although they may not mean much to you now, they may be helpful to return to once you've read the complete explanation of these techniques in Chapter 5.

1. **Poor Controls:** Often, children are unable by themselves to control their impulses or delay gratification. We tend to think of young children in this regard, but poor inner controls exist across the age span. For example, many teenagers do not have the internal strength to withstand peer pressure. Children of all ages with developmental disabilities often have poor control over self-stimulatory behavior such as rocking, head banging, and twirling. When poor control is your theory, it is important to provide external controls, such as monitoring, reminding, and penalizing techniques, to compensate for the lack of internal controls.

2. **Lack of Understanding or Ability:** Children can behave in negative ways because of certain limitations. Sometimes the limitations are cognitive. A child is limited in his ability to understand what is desired. Other times the limitations are physical. A child is unable to physically do what is wanted.

And sometimes the limitations are due to differing values. A child does not feel the same way as his parents about something. In each instance, the solution lies in teaching and rewarding rather than scolding.

3. **Avoidance:** Sometimes children are seeking a way to avoid something they dislike or fear. Their strategy usually involves negative behaviors that discourage their parents from proceeding. When avoidance is the goal, one of two parental responses is indicated. Either parents should proceed directly with the task at hand (regardless of the child's protests) or parents should encourage the behavior in a gradual manner. Ignoring tactics are helpful in the first course of action and encouraging can be tried in the second.

4. **Lack of Self-Worth:** When children do not feel good about themselves, a whole variety of problem behaviors ensue. Rudolf Dreikurs, one of the most widely read child psychologists, wrote that children try to feel worthwhile in three different ways: (1) by seeking excessive attention (I'm somebody if attention is paid to me all the time); (2) by seeking unwarranted power and control (I'm somebody if I can boss people around); and (3) by seeking revenge (I'm somebody if I can hurt people). When none of these outlets is possible, children usually seek failure (I'm already inadequate so nobody can expect me to be somebody). The implications of Dreikurs's theory are clear. Parents should sometimes avoid giving attention when children seek it and instead give attention on their own initiative. They should also avoid power struggles that feed a child's inflated sense of power and withstand children's attempts at humiliation and hurt. Techniques such as requesting and backing off are especially helpful. At the same time, parents need to be active in promoting self-reliant skills that enable children to find a healthy sense of well-being. A technique such as charting is recommended.

5. **Parental Reinforcement:** In addition to these four major "causes" of poor behavior, one more deserves special mention. Children are often difficult because they are encouraged to be difficult! We

seldom reinforce negative behavior deliberately, but nonetheless unintentionally encourage it on many occasions. The most common example is the failure to ignore temper tantrums, whining, and arguments. Every time we scream, act annoyed, or argue back, we run the risk of rewarding negative behavior instead of squelching it. That's because we often reach a point with our children where receiving negative attention (e.g., yelling) is better to them than getting no positive attention. In addition, parents may promote negative behavior in a child (again unconsciously) as a way to avoid conflict between each other. Many people resist this notion when they first hear about it because it is too painful to accept. What often happens is that it is far "safer" to battle a child than to battle a spouse. At the very least, it is possible to battle a spouse *through a child* rather than do it directly. There is the further possibility that one parent secretly encourages negative behavior to meet a special need. For example, when the youngest child has grown up and is about to "leave home," a parent becomes anxious over losing the "job" of parent. And so again without realizing it, the parent reinforces negative behavior (e.g., dependency, addictions) to stay "employed." Or a parent may unwittingly encourage negative behavior to involve the help of the other parent (who is otherwise distant) because the parent feels alone and isolated.

Consider the basic reasons children are difficult that I have just presented and think how they block your child's ability to change.

- Does your child have poor self-control?
- Is your child able to understand or physically carry out what you expect?
- Is your child trying to avoid certain experiences through misbehavior?
- Does your child use negative behavior to bolster self-esteem?
- Have you unconsciously encouraged your child's negative behavior?

WAITING FOR CHILDREN TO CHANGE

It is very tempting as a parent to wait for your child to change. By this I mean the hope that, sometime in the future, your child will decide to stop certain behavior and start others *on his own*.

I sometimes joke that every parent's prayer is "I hope it's just a stage" and every teacher's prayer is "I hope they grow up over the summer." Children do pass through stages, have good summers, and find a way to be different, but we are relying solely on time and good luck if we "leave the child alone."

In this book, you will read about several ways to seize the initiative—in effect, for you to make a change first in order for your child to make the next change. I realize all too well why it is difficult to be an active agent of change. In my experience, there are four reasons we wait for a child to make the first move.

1. **Sympathy:** We feel sorry for the difficulties our child may have and hold back pushing for change.

2. **Energy:** It's in short supply these days, and by now we realize that it will take a lot of energy to be consistent and persistent.

3. **Democracy:** We hold on to the mistaken notion that families are democracies and that it is unfair to push our child to do what she doesn't want to do.

4. **Guilt:** We've already made some mistakes raising our child and feel badly about them. We're concerned that we may damage our child further.

Keep in mind, however, all the benefits your child will reap if you believe he can change and take the first steps to help that change.

Your child will feel more secure.

Your child will be better liked.

Your child will not be spoiled.

Your child will be more self-reliant.

So lessen your feelings of sympathy and pangs of guilt, realize that you are the person in charge, and find the energy to persevere.

Questions and Answers

1. *You have been stressing the importance of expecting more from children. Don't some parents expect too much from their children?*

   Yes, some do and that pressure may be adversely affecting their child. However, it's been my experience that parents whose children have difficulties tend to expect too little.

2. *I've been urged to accept my child's handicap. Are you telling me the opposite?*

   If your child cannot do any more or any better than she currently has the resources to do, you should accept your child's limitations. For example, if the prognosis were that your child will never walk, or hear or see, not helping her to accept this fact would be unfair. But be sure you're not babying your child. Even children with handicaps can do more than they usually exhibit.

3. *You suggested trying new approaches with your child to find out what the problem may be. Is that using your child as a guinea pig?*

   To the contrary, it shows your willingness to find a way to help your child change.

4. *How do you help a very young child or a nonverbal child to understand what you want?*

   Use simple commands, gestures, and physical prompts to help the child do what you want. Also, if you act to reward or punish a behavior, the child will learn from your actions.

5. *Don't some children simply have a personality that can't be changed?*

   Children are born with different temperaments but their personality is not fixed at birth or even by six years of age. Personality changes can occur throughout the life cycle.

6. *I believe my child can change but I can't.*

   I won't accept that. Adults may not be as flexible as children but they have the resources to make bigger changes than children.

PART TWO

The Four-Step Plan

3

Step 1:
Get Clear What
You Want

The four-step plan is designed to help parents become an important agent of change for their children. The first step toward helping your child change is to get clear where *you* stand. The more certain you are about the things you expect and don't expect from your child, the less power he has to upset you.

What's your position on such matters as:

A fixed naptime	Disturbing parents
Bedtime	during the night
Chores to be done	Cursing
The whereabouts	Telephone use
of your child	An allowance
Sweets	Spending time with
Curfews	the family
Homework	How your child
TV usage	spends money
Sibling fights	The use of a car
Carrying your child	Putting possessions away

Needless to say, I could list hundreds of issues. Moreover, each issue has its subparts. For example, when is homework to be done? Where? How well? With how much help? Little wonder we can act confused and uncertain so often with children, but it is just such indecisiveness that causes us to lose control and not be in charge.

> Sally complained that her twelve-year-old daughter Susan was constantly on the phone. "It's really very stupid," Sally told me. "She and her friends call each other as soon as they get home from school." When asked what she wanted of Susan instead, Sally retorted: "To stay off the phone!" Sally was then asked to clarify her position: When could Susan use the phone? How long per call? What if Susan is not the caller? Are you open to a call-waiting feature on your phone line? Under what conditions would Sally allow a separate phone line? It took time for Sally to decide how she wanted to answer these questions, but once she did, Sally realized how unclear she had been and was eager to tell Susan the new telephone "rules."

Sometimes, the issue may have been clear before but not at the present time.

> Dave and Alice had a two-and-a-half-year-old son who had shown little interest in toilet training. They made a clear decision to postpone toilet training for three months. During that time no demands were made, diapers were changed willingly, and parents and child were relaxed. When it was time to resume, however, Dave and Alice were not clear about their objectives. Were they still going to let their child decide if he was not "interested"? What if he still resisted? Was he expected to sit on the toilet at certain times of the day? If so, for how long? Were training pants to be used exclusively during the day? Was the child to be rewarded for success? These questions (and several others) did not get answered before Dave and Alice began. They simply crossed their fingers and plunged ahead, varying their approach day by day as frustration mounted.

I am not suggesting that merely getting clear in your mind what you want will automatically lead to a change in your child's behavior. Naturally, resistance can occur to even the most carefully thought-out decisions. However, the more you know what you want, the easier it is to find a way to obtain it.

There are several important considerations to keep in mind while you are trying to clarify your thinking:

1. There is a difference between *wishing* and *insisting* that a behavior changes. Decide how strongly you feel about a change at the present time.

2. Your position does not have to be *strict* to be clear. It's perfectly all right to make a decision not to enforce a curfew or a TV viewing policy so long as you're clear that it's okay with you.

3. Your position does not have to be *permanent* to be clear. For instance, you can decide to outlaw sibling fights for one week to see how feasible that policy is. (Just don't change your mind every other day. That's "inconsistent.")

4. Don't expect to get clear about all the issues that arise with your children. You won't have time! But do select some issues that get you very upset and take the time to sort out your feelings about them. (Don't hesitate to talk out these feelings with your spouse or any other adult involved with your child.)

Getting clear is a way to put yourself in the driver's seat rather than reacting without too much thought. The process enables you to anticipate problems and be prepared.

To begin this process, you can start by filling out the list on the next page. Consider your children's living habits, relationships, responsibilities, and privileges and list the things that get you upset. Although I have previously suggested that you choose the child who is the greatest concern to you, you can do this exercise again if you have more than one child. If you wish, complete this form together with your co-parent. Leave the column "Grade" blank.

Things My Child Does That Get Me Upset   Grade

1. _____ _____

2. _____ _____

3. _____ _____

4. _____ _____

5. _____ _____

Now imagine that each one of the events on your list will happen again. How clear are you about your stand? Does your child *know* what you want? Give yourself a grade for each item on the list. Here is the grading system to use.

1 = *Clarity is inadequate.* I'm quite unsure what I would want and might even totally change my mind several times. My child would certainly be confused about where I stand.

2 = *Clarity is somewhat weak.* I have a lot more to think through about my position and my child may be somewhat confused also.

3 = *Clarity is good.* I know basically where I would stand on this matter, but I haven't figured out all the details. My child would have a good idea of what I want.

4 = *Clarity is very high.* I know where I would stand on this matter and my child would understand exactly what I expect from him.

Next, pick out *one* item that you believe needs greater clarity. Write it down and think about each of the questions that follows. Some may be easy to answer; others may be difficult. Do your best.

I NEED TO BE CLEARER ABOUT:

_____

_____

_____

_____

_____

_____

QUESTIONS TO HELP ME GET CLEARER:

1. Do I really want to pursue a change in this behavior *at this time*?

   (If you do, proceed with the next questions. If you don't, postpone the matter for a later time. Decide if you would like to pursue another behavior instead.)

2. What specifically do I want to see changed?

3. Can my child take any small first steps in the direction of getting what I want? Would I be willing to pursue only these smaller steps for now? Or do I want the entire situation improved?

4. Do I expect my child to make changes by herself? How much help am I willing to give my child to obtain the desired behavior?

5. Do other adults (spouse, relatives, teachers, etc.) have the same objectives as I do?

Answering these questions should help you to become clearer and more decisive. Here is an example of how a parent was helped by coming to grips with these questions.

Margaret had been quite concerned about the junk food she was allowing her seven-year-old daughter to eat. An interviewer asked her the preceding five questions and this is how she replied:

Interviewer: Is this problem something you really want to deal with this coming week?

Margaret: Yes, it's waited long enough.

Interviewer: What specifically do you want to see changed?

Margaret: I'd like my daughter to stop drinking and eating sugar-sweetened foods.

Interviewer: Would you be willing to start by prohibiting some of these foods or do you want her to stop consuming all sugared foods and drinks?

Margaret: Well, I'd really like to see it all stopped.

Interviewer: Is this just wishful thinking or something you're going to insist on?

Margaret: I insist that the drinks have to stop. I can live with sweetened cereal for a while, but it's the soda and sweetened juices that are really getting me upset.

Interviewer: Do you expect your daughter to make the changes by herself?

Margaret: What do you mean?

Interviewer: Do you want to tell her she cannot have soda or sweetened juices anymore and that's that *or* do you want to help her with the change? For example, you could go to the store with her and offer to buy the 100 percent juices of her choice? I'm not suggesting that going to the store is the right idea. I'm just trying to understand what it is you want.

Margaret: That's a hard one. (Pause) No, I think I will just tell her and buy the 100 percent juices myself. I don't want to make a big production out of it.

Interviewer: Okay. My last question is, does your husband agree with you about this?

Margaret: In general he does, but he doesn't seem to care about it as much as I do. I guess I should tell him exactly where I stand and see if he's willing to support me.

Interviewer: Yes, that's a good idea. Even if he doesn't want to support you strongly, he may be willing to not interfere with your efforts. Or maybe he's got other thoughts about it. Talk to him before you make a final decision.

Sometimes we are afraid to take a different position than the one we are accustomed to. In this case, it is helpful to consider a change. Notice in the interview that follows how the interviewer helps a parent through this process.

When Sylvia dropped her three-year-old son Alex at a day-care center every day, he clung to her and didn't want her to leave. Sylvia usually stayed there for up to fifteen minutes. Often that didn't do the trick and she had to leave despite Alex's protests. After she left, Alex always settled down and had an enjoyable day.

Interviewer: Do you want to continue remaining with Alex for fifteen minutes every day?

Sylvia: I'm not sure. I just think he's a little insecure these days and is asking for my reassurance.

Interviewer: How do you know that Alex needs this reassurance? Are you giving it just because he asks for it?

Sylvia: I guess so because he's fine after I leave.

Interviewer: That's right . . . Maybe he's just testing *you*. Would you be willing to test *him*? Would you like to see if he can do without your reassurance?

Sylvia: Okay. What should I do?

Interviewer: Why not take the position that you are going to stay no more than five minutes and will leave him whether or not he is settled? You can try it on "for size" for one week and see if it's a good position. If you don't like the results, you can always change again.

Sylvia: Do you think it will work?

Interviewer: I can't say, but it is clear that Alex needs to find his own way to adjust to your leaving him. Staying with him for fifteen minutes doesn't help him do that. In fact, it may only reassure you, not him.

Sylvia: I hadn't thought of it that way. I think I'll give it a try.

As you try to get clearer with your child, consider the following suggestions:

1. Don't "feel out" your child's response to your wishes next time, gingerly suggesting what you'd like and waiting to see how he responds. Make up your mind beforehand. There's a big difference between "Are you getting tired?" and "It's time to go to bed."

2. Establish in your mind whether you are willing to give your child plenty of time to change her behavior or whether you want quick results. Either choice is okay so long as it's the position you are willing to accept. If you decide on a gradual change, set a date in your mind when you want to achieve full results.

3. Figure out the specific behaviors you want from your child and go over them slowly so that your child knows as well. By all means, demonstrate the behaviors if your child is young and even practice them if possible.

4. Examine how you might confuse your child by the way you respond to his behavior. For example, if you scream about a child's unacceptable behavior and do nothing else, the child should conclude that you really don't expect him to change. Inconsistency is another way to confuse.

5. On matters for which you are really unsure what stand to take, experiment for a week with a particular position and see how it feels. Don't get frozen by indecisiveness. When you ride the fence, you'll never learn where you want to stand. Don't worry if you decide to change your mind. Your child will see you as thoughtful rather than indecisive.

Questions and Answers

1. *What expectations should I have for my child?*

   Those are your decisions as a parent! I can no more tell you whether a seven-year-old should be told to make his own bed than whether a seventeen-year-old should be told that she is too young to be sexually active. I have my preferences like anybody else (for one thing, I don't think that parents should fuss over whether kids eat vegetables), but they are for my kids, not yours. By all means, however, talk with friends and relatives. You don't have to agree with them but their opinions may be helpful.

2. *What if a parent makes a decision that turns out to be very poor?*

   My feeling is that there are acceptable risks in parenting that can be tolerated by children. The decision can always be changed. For example, to force a child to do homework right after school may turn out to be a bad idea. However, the failure to attempt such a policy in the first place may mean that a good decision as to when homework is done is never discovered.

3. *Isn't it important to find out what your child wants, at least some of the time, instead of always thinking about what you, as a parent, want?*

   Of course we should listen to our children and consider their wishes. But as I pointed out in the case of the child who won't let his mother leave him at day care, we need to make our best judgments a lot about what our kids can handle. We need to test their limits sometimes instead of always having our limits tested by them.

4. *Can you take a stand that none of the other parents in the neighborhood seems to be taking?*

Yes. You'd be surprised how many other parents are aching to say no to many things their kids want, but don't feel they have the support. If you can, talk to your neighbors and the parents of your children's friends. You might be surprised. In my daughter's high school, for example, parents have succeeded in establishing a safe, nondrinking post-prom party. A few years ago, there was total despair that any parents cared about the drunk driving that occurred.

5. *I can't see what good it is to get clear about a behavior you're not going to get anyhow. Am I missing something?*

Sure, many changes you might want to see will be difficult to get. The key is to get clear what is the first step you want from your child, not the last. I know someone who got clear that he wanted his cursing son to eliminate just one foul word from his vocabulary, even though he objected to many others. Starting small, this father was eventually successful in helping his son make considerable changes.

4

Step 2:
Remain Calm
and Confident

"When I tell my seventeen-year-old to do something," one mother told me, "She replies, 'Don't worry about it!' Inevitably, I get very upset and we end up in a screaming match. I realize that she can easily get me into an argument and I try to control myself. I even stop talking to her, and yet, it ends up, she'll get me to blow up."

If I told this mother "Calm down!" how successful would she be?

The truth is that few people can "calm down" just be being told to do so or even by making their own personal resolution to relax. It takes a lot more.

This truth applies particularly to parents when children are difficult. As one well-known joke goes: "Nervous breakdowns are hereditary . . . they come from our children!" It takes a kind of patient saint to stay calm in the face of sloppiness, forgetfulness, and selfishness displayed day in and day out.

While there is no complete cure (nor should there be) for becoming very angry or overreacting to children's behavior, one thing is clear. Unless stressed parents can find a way to act and react with some degree of calmness, they will not show their children that they are both *in charge* and *involved*. Instead, they will seem hysterical or scary.

Staying calm and confident has two specific benefits. First, it allows you to maintain some control over your reactions and your responses in conflict situations with children. By being more in charge of yourself, your children are less likely to "push your emotional buttons"—those nasty little cues that make you feel guilty, inadequate, or perhaps enraged. Second, it helps your children gain some control over themselves—your calmness invites them to be calmer (and hopefully, more mature).

Because you cannot simply will yourself to respond calmly and confidently, I would like to share with you several tips on how to stay calm and confident which you can try out with your children. Before launching into these suggestions, one matter needs to be clear. I'm not recommending that parents should never be emotional or downright angry at their children. Heaven knows, children were not meant to be raised by robots. Also, by holding in our emotions too long, our feelings often accumulate, and when we do lose control it is way out of proportion to the situation. But acknowledging this fact does not give us a license to "let it all hang out." We have a responsibility to give children a mature example of how conflict can be resolved. There is also no guarantee that displays of calmness and confidence will always get you what you want. Children can be stubborn no matter how perfectly we express ourselves. But I do assure you that you can avoid a lot of defiance by the way you come across with children.

TALKING AND BEHAVING CONFIDENTLY

There are three different styles most parents use to express their authority: (1) pleading; (2) angry; and (3) confident. In the chart that follows, these three styles are compared.

Pleading	Angry	Confident
Try to be nice	Blow up in anger	Make clear, direct requests
Act flustered	Argue endlessly	Reveal honest feelings
Question too much	Accuse	Give brief reasons
Beg	Get into power struggles	Persist

Pleading	Angry	Confident
Are confusing, unclear	Discredit children's thinking	Politely refuse to do something
Let yourself be treated unfairly	Trick, tease, put down	Empathize
Worry about being popular	Give harsh punishments	Follow through with reasonable consequences
Are afraid of upsetting children	Nag	Listen to children's point of view
Blame yourself	Withhold information about what you expect	Don't allow yourself to be rushed

Rarely does a parent stay with one style exclusively. A typical pattern is for a parent to begin pleading and then get so frustrated that she switches to anger. Notice how this switch occurs in the following three examples.

Mother to five-year-old girl at restaurant: "Do you want milk?"

Daughter: Coke!

Mother: (pleading) How about milk? You haven't had milk in two weeks!

Daughter: (defiantly) I want Coke!

Mother: (sweetly) Give me a kiss.

Daughter: No!

Mother: But Mommy gives you kisses all the time. Please?

Daughter: I hate you.

Mother: (quite angry now) Well, if that's how mean you want to be to your mommy, you can forget Coke! You're such a baby!

Daughter: (crying) I want Coke.

Mother: You're going to get a spanking instead.

Father to his ten-year-old son:
"It's after 9:30. You're still up?"

Son: Oh, Dad. Come on! All the good programs are between 9:00 and 10:00.

Father: (pleading) You always do this to me. We go through this every night. I'm so tired of it. Couldn't you go to bed when it's your bedtime?

Son: Dad, all my friends are watching the same program. It's not fair!

Father: Maybe they don't get up every morning as tired as you do.

Son: Don't you care what I'm telling you?

Father: (annoyed) Yeah, I care that you're driving me crazy! I can't stand this anymore.

Son: (emphatically) I'm not tired in the morning!

Father: (quite angry now) Yes, you are! And you're one big spoiled brat. Get upstairs before you get it!

A sixteen-year-old to his single-parent mother:
"A bunch of friends are going to New York. Can I go?"

Mother: (gingerly) You're too young to go to New York, don't you think?

Son: (bristling) Oh, come on, Mom. Don't start giving me a hard time.

Mother: (instantly angry) I don't even want to hear about it!

Son: (talking very quickly) Mom, there are so many neat things to do in the Village and everybody else is getting to go. And I'm sick of staying home all the time!

Mother: You only think about yourself. I work all day long and come home tired, and you want me to stay up all night worrying about you in New York.

Son: Stop worrying, Mom.

Mother: How can I with a son like you!

Instead of these struggles, a confident style allows a parent to appear calm and assertive and is less susceptible to power struggles. You can practice certain key skills to develop a consistently confident style.

Being Direct

You will appear more confident when you are straightforward in your dealings with children. Use phrases like *"I'd like . . .* (the toys to be put away before you watch TV)," *"Your job . . .* (is to keep the kitchen clean)," *"The rule is . . .* (no hitting)," *"I will not . . .* (buy sugar-coated cereal)." With very young children or children with communication handicaps, it's especially important to use simple instructions (without changing your words each time) such as "No biting" or "Look at me." Being direct does not take a lot of communication skills. Avoid such questions as "How about a thank you?" or "Don't you think you're tired?" Rhetorical appeals may preserve a "nice guy" image but almost never get results. Likewise, accusatory statements such as "You don't even care" or "Don't you think you're being a big baby?" only make children want to get back at you.

To help you avoid such remarks, I recommend that you *focus on what you expect* from your child whenever he is doing something unacceptable. Often, there is a tendency to *comment on a child's behavior* instead. A comment such as "You're being a pain," for example, is far less direct than a statement such as "You are to leave me alone and take care of yourself."

Commenting on our child's behaviors often happens because we are uncomfortable about owning up to our feelings of anger. Instead of talking directly about our anger, we often cover it by accusing someone.

> For example, assume it's Sunday and a brother and sister, Joel and Debby, are playing so noisily that they wake up their baby sister in the middle of her daily nap. They know how important it is to be quiet in the vicinity of the baby's room but lately have been quite forgetful about this. Their father, Marty, is livid (especially because it's his turn at child care) and yells out, "How many times do you need to be

told to keep quiet during the baby's nap? You're both totally self-centered." Marty would have been better off saying more directly, "Now that the baby is awake, my afternoon is loused up and I just really resent it. The two of you are going to have to play with the baby now that she's up and needs to be taken care of."

Of course, it's not always possible to remember to be direct. It's so easy to lapse into expressions of exasperation when we see something we don't like or nervous okays after we ask for something we think will be refused. But it may be possible to catch yourself and *switch* to more direct language. If you do, you'll be surprised how much calmer (and confident) you'll be.

Watching Body Language

Children pick up subtle things in a parent's body language that suggest they can grab the upper hand. Establishing eye contact when you state your wishes to your children is critical. It also is especially important to make sure that your face backs up what you are saying. Saying "I want you to stop" with a pleading grin won't get the message across. You can sometimes avoid a lot of power struggles by giving instructions or refusing unreasonable requests without *any* talking. Giving directions with simple hand gestures or stopping mischief by shaking your head no is often more effective than a bunch of words.

Children are bundles of energy and want action to go quickly. Learn to slow them down by your own physical calmness. For example, move slowly (but without hesitation) into a room in which siblings are fighting. When you race to the scene of action, your adrenaline is flowing, you're out of breath, and you will probably overreact.

With young children, it is important to communicate in a physical manner. Hold toddlers firmly for a minute or two if they run away and bite or get into other trouble. Also, guide them hand over hand through activities such as putting on clothes, but be careful not to do it for them. Try removing your hands slightly and see if your child does it alone. Also try holding your child's hand less and less as you walk together.

Showing Interest

Many parents believe that they will lose in a conflict if they listen or show sympathy for the child's point of view. In actuality, they are showing the child that they lack confidence in their own ability to judge a situation on its merits by changing their minds if warranted or sticking to their guns if needed.

A parent once called in to a radio program on which I was a guest and said, "I tell my twelve-year-old son he has to stop fighting with his sister but he continues to argue, saying, 'You just don't want to hear what I have to say, do you?' I'll say, 'No, I don't.' And then he'll say, 'You just don't care about my feelings, do you?' and I'll say, 'No, I don't.' Then he'll get frustrated, burst into tears, and run up to his room and slam the door. At this point, I really feel like killing him but then I try to understand that, in his mind, he thinks he's right. I don't know how to handle it." I asked: "Is he right that you don't hear him out?" And she responded, "Sometimes." I continued, "You can probably risk hearing him a lot more. You can say to yourself, *I can be a parent who will listen.* If he is persuasive, tell him that you'll give a lot of consideration to what he's saying. If he doesn't sway you, you can say, 'I've given you a good hearing. I'm really glad you shared all your feelings with me. I still expect you to fight less with your sister.'"

There are three ways you can show a reasonable degree of interest in your child's point of view: *checking out, empathizing,* and *acknowledging. Checking out* is asking for clarification of what your child is saying or feeling. For example, let's assume that your child is very upset about going to visit a relative and you're not sure why. You might say, "I'm not sure why you're not willing to go. Tell me some of your feelings and I'll listen." *Empathizing* is expressing understanding of your children's feelings. When your child doesn't want to come in for dinner, you might empathize, "I know you'd rather keep playing, but dinner is ready." *Acknowledging* is recognizing the validity of your child's point of view. Assume you have told your teenager that you are not sure if he can go to an unsupervised party and the teenager responds, "I can be trusted." If you agree that this is probably so, you might respond, "I think you can be trusted but I'm still not sure you should go. I want you to try to convince me that there will be no problems there before I give you my permission."

DEALING WITH CHILDREN'S PROTESTS

Nothing is more draining and more likely to cause you to lose control than your children's continual protests to your requests or decisions (even if you show some interest in their feelings). Here is some advice to help you cope and stay calm.

1. Give Reasons Nondefensively

When children protest, they can be given a brief, respectful, honest explanation why the request is being made, as in "I don't want you to watch that TV program because I think it teaches very wrong ideas about how people should solve problems." Too often, however, parents go on and on justifying themselves as if their stand is not justifiable until their children agree with them (they seldom do).

Parent: I think it teaches very wrong ideas about how people should solve problems.

Child: Oh, come on! It's just a very funny program.

Parent: But it does have a lot of killing.

Child: So what! You worry too much.

Parent: *But don't you think that it can affect you without your realizing it?*

Child: No I don't.

The parent, in this situation, would be a lot better off stating, "I do worry about your watching it and that's why you can't."

2. Enjoy the Pause That Refreshes

Don't be afraid to say things such as "Let me think about it and I will tell you in a few minutes" or "Your dad and I will talk about it and tell you tomorrow."

Parents often have the notion that they have to respond instantly to children's pressure. As a result, they wind up talking too much and acting too fast. Allowing children to rush you will only allow them to get you upset. When you're upset, you may become tense and start to yell, scream, or hit. Take time to clarify thoughts and decisions, especially when you're unsure where you stand or you've given a quick response under pressure and would like the time to rethink matters. If your eventual decision turns out to be unpopular with your child, so be it.

3. Don't Get Sidetracked

Children have ways to get you off the topic by (1) saying things like "That's not fair," "You just don't understand," or "Don't you trust me?"; or (2) behaving quite distressed—either crying, creating temper tantrums, or just sulking. One of the best ways to fend off these maneuvers is to calmly repeat what you want like a broken record, as in "It's your bedtime." Of course, it isn't easy to repeat this message as an uninterested six-year-old continues to play with toys, or when a child says that she is thirsty or hungry or begs for "five more minutes." Nor is it easy to repeat the same message without raising your voice. Yet "It's you bedtime," repeated slowly each time a child protests, can be remarkably effective with even the most argumentative children.

Another technique to add to your arsenal is quick responses to children's protests, such as "That may be," "That's not what we're talking about," or "Sometimes, it isn't fair," followed by a repetition of your instructions. This can be illustrated by the following dialogue:

Parent: Billy, it's 9:30, time to get to bed.

Billy: I'm not tired!

Parent: That may be, but it's time to go to sleep. Get into your pajamas.

Billy: It's not fair. All my friends don't have such an early bedtime.

Parent: Sometimes I'm not fair, but it's time to go to bed.

Billy: Just because I go to bed doesn't mean I can fall asleep!

Parent: You're right, but no more arguments. It's time to go to bed.

Whenever your child balks at your wishes (and you've already given an adequate hearing of his point of view), the important thing is to *hold the line*, taking the knocks along the way.

Remember the teenager who wants to go to New York. Here is how his mother might hold the line and take the knocks:

Son: I'm going to New York Saturday night with a bunch of kids.

Mother: Wait a minute. This is the first time I've heard about it and I have a hard time with "I'm going." Tell me about what's going on and then we'll discuss whether you can go.

Son: Look, a bunch of kids made arrangements to go to the Village and I really want to go, Mom. And I don't want you to say no to me.

Mother: Are there any adults going with you?

Son: Well, there's this college student. He knows the Village scene and he said he would go.

Mother: Well, I certainly would be willing to think about this . . .

Son: (interrupts) I've got to give people an answer. I've got to call John up in ten minutes. They're depending on me. Come on, Mom!

Mother: No, I need more information than you're giving me.

Son: You're dragging my time out, Mom!

Mother: That may be. I need more information about who's going, when and how you're leaving, where you're going, and when you're coming home.

Son: You're being ridiculous!

Mother: That may be.

Son: Listen, you're lucky I'm even telling you. One of these days I'll just go without telling you.

Mother: That's not what we're talking about now. Get me the information and I'll decide if you can go.

Finally, the remaining option to cope with a child's protests is to simply ignore them and proceed with what needs to happen (a particularly useful method with young children). Thus, you might carry balking children to bed if they refuse to walk there or firmly hold the arms of a child who is hurting others by throwing toys. These direct methods are especially helpful for parents who don't feel that they are getting through to their young child. Again and again, you can see that being an effective parent to a child doesn't necessarily require advanced communication between parent and child; it requires quiet firmness and direction.

Older children, of course, cannot be handled so easily in a physical manner. When they balk, you can give them a clear choice: either compliance or a consequence you specify (e.g., unplugging the TV). If they continue to argue, you can assume that they have chosen the "consequence."

SHOWING CONFIDENCE IN YOUR CHILD

I'm a firm believer that sometimes when we want something from children we should convey our confidence that they can act maturely. Rather than ordering them to do something, we can, at times, ask them first if they are willing to cooperate. Even if we give children a chance to cooperate, however, they may not take us up on our offer. So I've developed a three-step strategy that covers all the possibilities.

1. As a first step, *invite* your child to cooperate. You can do this by saying, for example, "Are you ready to _____ ?" (For a child with limited communication, you can simply signal what you want for a response.) If you get a "no," consider it the *first refusal*.

2. As a second step, move closer to the child and ask again "Are you ready to _____ ?" or gesture more clearly what you want. If you still get a "no," consider it the *second refusal*.

3. As a third step, decide if you really want compliance. If you do, give a clear command and back it up if necessary with physical firmness or some consequence. If you decide to back off (which is a perfectly confident thing to do), walk away. You can always decide to return and begin the procedure again.

I have found that this three-step process works particularly well for young children. For example, assume you want to leave a friend's home or apartment. You can ask your child, "Are you ready to put your coat on?" and hold up the coat. If you get a first refusal, simply move closer to your child, ask again for cooperation, and place the coat sleeves in such a way that the child can be helped to put on the coat. Be sure to wait for your child to decide if he is going to cooperate. If you get a second refusal, you then have the possibility of putting the coat on forcefully or simply scooping up the child, coat in hand, and leaving regardless of his protests. (You can also stop on the way out and give your child another chance to act maturely.)

Most parents assume that their child will always hold out till the end when they become familiar with the routine. To the contrary, I have found that children are quite cooperative and mature once they are accustomed to the whole cycle.

I would not exclude older children from this procedure. For example, one could ask, "Are you ready to clean your room?" After a refusal, wait awhile (the time interval is up to you) and come back asking a second time, "Are you ready to clean your room? I really hope so because I have to vacuum it soon" (or give any other honest reason). After the second refusal, choose between backing off (for a far longer period of time) or taking an action such as placing everything on the floor in a laundry basket or insisting that the room be cleaned.

The best thing about the procedure is that even if you are not pleased with the results, your child has not succeeded in getting you upset or making you lose control.

Questions and Answers

1. *Is it really possible to stay calm with children, especially when they act up in public?*

   Naturally, staying calm with children is easier said than done. However, it's not hard to get better and better at it. Just taking a few moments to get clear in your mind what you want to accomplish in a given situation will already help to calm you. All the other suggestions you have just read are designed to make it possible to become calmer and more confident—

even in public. Also remember that you can prevent future occurrences by sending your child to her room as soon as you return home after a public spectacle.

2. *Shouldn't you yell at kids once in a while to let them know that you are angry at their behavior?*

   The key thing is to examine your own style. If you're a "screamer," it's really important to develop a quieter yet firm manner. But if you're typically soft-spoken (and your children are not as responsive to your requests as you would like), raising your voice, even yelling a bit, might be an important change of pace.

3. *What are the most important things to change in my nonverbal behavior?*

   I find the big ones are eye contact, voice speed/volume, touching, and signals. Approach children more directly and establish firm (but not scary) eye contact in making requests; alter your voice to be slower, faster, louder, or softer than it normally is; touch children affectionately more often to gain cooperation or hold them firmly to restrain them; give directions or say no with gestures rather than a bunch of words.

4. *Do you approve of spanking?*

   Spanking is a very individual matter. I caution you not to make it a habit because then you are teaching your children that "might makes right." Physical restraint is a good alternative to consider. It may do the job just as well as spanking.

5. *I tried your suggestions but my kids are still not disciplined. Isn't there more to changing children's behavior than staying calm?*

   The skills presented in this chapter are not really "discipline strategies." They are basic ways of responding to and confronting children which lay the foundation for the specific strategies in the next chapter. Read on!

5

Step 3: Select a Plan of Action

It's somewhat normal to think that problems your child poses cannot be resolved unless your child changes by himself. "It's only a phase" and "He'll grow up eventually" are really expressions that change is something only in your child's hands. But you can help your child change, maybe not in every respect but certainly in some.

The key to helping children change is for us adults to change *first*. We need to lead the way because we have the emotional maturity and wisdom our children lack. I'm not suggesting that it's you and I who are really at fault. It's unlikely that we have caused our children's problems, but we certainly are doing some things that help the problems to *persist*. If we don't try hard to change some of those behaviors, we are as big a "discipline" problem as our children.

The basic change we need to make is to shift from a *reactive* stance to a *proactive* one. When we are reactive, we await the next episode of problem behavior, without a plan of action, and then have to react by the seat of our pants. When we are proactive, we have anticipated the problems, have prepared a plan of action, and are more likely to be in the driver's seat.

SELECTING A PROBLEM BEHAVIOR

The first proactive step you can take is to select one behavior that is of particular concern to you and for which you are prepared to expend time and energy during the next week. You will be more effective if you choose one behavior because you will have a concrete goal to work toward. If you don't have a specific target, rest assured that your child will overwhelm and frustrate your efforts to help.

The activity on the next page will help you select a problem behavior. Begin your selection by writing down up to five problem behaviors exhibited by your child. Again, do this together with a partner, if appropriate. Be sure to list specific behaviors, not general things like "her attitude." You may wish to select behaviors from the following list.

Some Problem Behaviors of Children

Calls for me during
   the night
Runs away
Won't nap
Resists toilet training
Destroys property
Throws tantrums
Overeats; eats junk
Hits others
Wets bed
Teases siblings
Doesn't share toys
Doesn't wash, brush
   teeth, etc.
Leaves things to the
   last minute

Doesn't do chores
Lies
Won't do homework
   without help
Shows off and clowns
Won't communicate feelings
Refuses to be part of
   family events
Swears
Talks too much on phone
Watches too much TV
Speaks negatively about me
Steals
Dresses inappropriately
Experiments with drugs/
   alcohol

Problem Behaviors of My Child

1. _____

2. _____

3. _____

4. _____

5. _____

Now choose one as your target for next week. Some parents prefer to begin with the easiest one; others like to tackle the hard one right away. Put the four you don't select "on the back burner." You may need to cope with these four (and many more) during the next week but be sure to reserve special attention to the one you have put "on the front burner."

THE BEHAVIOR I CHOOSE TO WORK ON THIS WEEK IS:

_____

_____

_____

_____

You are now ready to develop a plan to help your child change a behavior.

EXPERIMENTING WITH NEW APPROACHES

The second proactive step you can take is to seriously experiment with a new approach to the problem behavior you have selected. No doubt, there is a characteristic approach you've taken to try to change the problem. Perhaps you've screamed a lot, or used a particular punishment, or tried a bribe. Maybe you think you've tried *everything*. (Could that be the problem?) Whatever the case, if you're not getting anywhere, it's time for something *new*. At the very least, STOP what you are doing . . . it's not working.

If you've read other books, you have no doubt been introduced to *the* method for changing your child. The trouble is that one book contradicts the other and the reader is left confused and bewildered.

Such a reader called in to another radio show on which I was a guest and poured forth:

> I'm twenty-nine and have two children. They're both girls, four-and-a-half and two-and-a-half. We're having a discipline problem with our four-and-a-half-year-old. She doesn't listen to us and the specific problem we're having is with her going into the street. I've read many books and I've gone to college, and I've done all these great things. I've tried to negotiate with her and we've established punishments, which she doesn't follow through with on her own. Then I have to think of a new punishment and she still winds up going out into the street again. For example, the neighbors came and told me that she was out in the street again yesterday. I sat down and instead of being angry with her and yelling, I said, "You were in the street," and she said, "Yes, I was," and I said, "What do you think we should do about this?" She said, "Well, I shouldn't be allowed to go outside for two days," and I said, "That sounds reasonable, but it would be more reasonable if you just don't go out into the street anymore." And she said, "Well, I won't." Sure enough, in the next half hour she did.

To counteract this confusion and contradictory advice, I propose to you the following: *There are ten basically different options a parent has to help a child change a behavior. Moreover, it often makes little difference which of these options are chosen. Merely shifting gears in your handling of the problem breaks the pattern that has been going on.* For example, if you have been *punitive* with your child and it hasn't gotten you anywhere, I encourage you to be *rewarding*. If you have always tried to *discuss* the problem with your child, why not try to *ignore* it? Any one method, in and of itself, may be effective or ineffective. The important thing is for you to have an alternative plan when the one you have been using doesn't serve you any longer.

> Sally and Ken, for instance, had three children: sixteen, fourteen, and ten. For years all three had the habit of leaving items where they didn't belong (e.g., school bags in the doorways, dirty dishes in the living room, newspapers and magazines left where they were read). Whenever Sally and Ken found something left where it didn't belong, they inquired who's responsible and had the offender correct the situation immediately. Although the children complied with this demand without much fuss, their habits had not changed. They still left things even if they had to correct the matter later. Since this pattern had been going on for several years, Sally and Ken were getting quite tired by their own efforts and finally realized that the problem had never been solved satisfactorily.

Sally and Ken had been using what I would call a *monitoring* approach to their problem. It's a perfectly good idea (and it's included in the list of ten options), but it wasn't helping. Now is the time to develop another approach. Let me tell you nine other plans they might use to get their concerns across:

1. Sally and Ken could call a family meeting. They could ask their children to hammer out an agreement with them containing firm commitments about picking up after themselves. The results could be reviewed a week later (REQUESTING).

2. Signs could be posted at the door reminding the children to put their belongings away immediately. For one week, the rules concerning picking up after oneself could be stated each morning at breakfast (REMINDING).

3. All comments and instructions about leaving messes could be stopped for one week. Although messes might accumulate, it's

possible the children will become more aware of their habits without adults around to monitor them (IGNORING).

4. A chart that keeps a count of all the things left around (by all three children) could be posted on the refrigerator for one week. The results could be discussed with the children (CHARTING).

5. Each child could earn the right to rent a video of her choice if there was solid improvement in putting things away over the course of one week (REWARDING).

6. All negative comments about the children concerning their habits could be curtailed for one week. Instead, Sally and Ken could express their hope that the children will change their ways and could praise *any* positive steps they take (ENCOURAGING).

7. Sally and Ken could take each child on a tour of the house, pointing out where things tend to be left. Suggestions might be given for ways to remember to put things away. The consequences to the rest of the family when belongings are left around could be discussed (TEACHING).

8. The children can be told that their parents are getting tired of monitoring the situation and that, for one week, it will be the children's responsibility to monitor themselves (BACKING OFF).

9. Each child will be fined 50 cents from their weekly allowance for each item left where it doesn't belong at a designated time each night (PENALIZING).

I hope you are impressed by all the options Sally and Ken have! It's my belief that several of the approaches (singly or in combination) would be successful in changing the situation because they *break the pattern* of parents' monitoring and children correcting. Each one represents a serious change in how Sally and Ken approach their children.

I also suspect that you have many reservations about my suggestions for Sally and Ken. For example, what if your children don't care about videos (or you don't have a VCR)? What if you don't give *your* children an allowance? More importantly, what if *your* children accuse each other of leaving the mess? While I could go on and on anticipating your questions, let's instead examine the ten basic options more closely.

THE TEN BASIC OPTIONS IN CHANGING CHILDREN'S BEHAVIOR

The ten basic options are listed below to assist you in creating plans. Any one of these options may serve you well, or you may wish to combine a few of them into one plan.

1. **REQUESTING**
   You bring your concerns to the child and ask him to alter the behavior.

2. **REMINDING**
   You remind your child on a daily basis of a rule you have established.

3. **MONITORING**
   You stay with a child to make sure your wishes are fulfilled or you make frequent checks on her behavior.

4. **IGNORING**
   You do not respond to a child's negative behavior, giving attention only when the behavior stops.

5. **CHARTING**
   You or your child keeps a record of positive or negative behaviors.

6. **REWARDING**
   You inform the child that a positive behavior will be reinforced by some tangible reward.

7. **ENCOURAGING**
   You maintain a positive view of your child and compliment any actions that are steps toward the desired results.

8. **TEACHING**
   You discuss and demonstrate to your child the behavior you expect and, if warranted, practice it with him.

9. **BACKING OFF**
   You shift gears on the child by temporarily giving up your expectations.

10. **PENALIZING**
    You establish a negative consequence for the child's misbehavior.

As you consider and implement these options, it is imperative to keep in mind the following points:

1. Avoid using the same option over and over again. Select from the ones you have rarely used in the past. The more you are willing to change your approach, the more your child will be able to change her behavior.

2. Make a commitment to stick to your plan for one or two weeks to determine its effectiveness. Think of your plan as a serious experiment in helping your child to change his behavior.

3. If you share parenting duties with a mate, grandparent, etc., obtain their support (or, at the least, noninterference) in carrying out your plan. The best approach is to include the other "parent" in creating the action plan.

4. Make sure your action plan deals with changing a specific problem behavior. If you attempt to change an attitude, disposition, "phase" your child is going through, or any other vague target, you are bound to fail.

5. The way you conduct yourself in carrying out a plan is often more important than the details of the plan itself. Talk and behave calmly and confidently. If you are pleading or angry, the plan will not be effective. Most plans should be presented to a child before they take effect. A confident attitude and style on your part in this initial presentation is most helpful.

6. KEEP TO YOUR PLAN. The more disciplined you are about carrying out your plan, the more disciplined your children will be in the future.

To help you understand exactly what is entailed in each of the options, I will discuss each one in considerable detail.

Option 1: Requesting

It's amazing how often parents assume that undesirable behaviors can be changed only if they tell their children what has to happen. *Requesting* involves asking, not telling. Rather than setting down the law themselves, parents can use the alternative of bringing their concerns to their children and requesting them to work out a plan for altering the problem. This is a perfectly confident procedure so long as parents approach children with the attitude that nothing has been lost if the request is refused. Parents can then take a more "take charge" approach.

What to Do

1. Approach your child and state what he does that needs to change (e.g., "You go to bed without finishing your chores").
2. Ask him, "Are you willing to change this situation?" If the answer is yes, ask, "What are you willing to do?"

If your child makes an acceptable offer (e.g., "I will do all my chores before I start my homework"), respond with words like "I appreciate your promise and I am counting on you to keep it." (A handshake or a simple hug would be in order!) More than likely, you will get a vague promise to change. Accept it, but also press for a more specific commitment (e.g., "When will you agree to have your chores done tonight?"). If your child wants to strike a bargain with you, you have the right to accept or refuse. If your child resists your invitation to change his behavior, try repeating the invitation: "No, I really mean it. Are you willing to take responsibility for this or do you want me to get involved?" If you still get nowhere, then dismiss him with a request to think over the conversation and return to the discussion at a time you think appropriate. You can repeat this procedure for several days before abandoning it.

Case Examples

1. Jim had been upset for a long time that his fourteen-year-old son picked on his ten-year-old sister unmercifully. When his son was younger, Jim usually sent him to his room when things got really out of hand. Since his son became a teenager, Jim had no plan of action. He was advised to use a *requesting* approach. In a meeting with his son, this dialogue ensued:

   Father: This business with your sister is getting out of hand. It's getting the whole family upset. What would you be willing to do to change the situation?

   Son: My treatment of her is perfectly fair because she bothers me just to annoy me, and on the whole, she's a total nuisance.

Father: That could be. I don't want to turn this into a court of who's right and who's wrong. I want you to answer my question, What would you be willing to do to change the situation?

Son: Why can't we fight? I don't butt into your fights.

Father: That's true . . . but I still want to ask you, What would you be willing to do to change the situation?

Son: Well, I suppose I could tell her what bothers me rather than getting so upset, but if she keeps doing it I'm going to take action! I don't have to tolerate her!

Father: I heard something that was encouraging. You said that you would be willing to explain to her how she bothers you.

Son: Yeah.

Father: Would you like my suggestions about how to do that or do you want to handle it yourself?

Son: I think I can do it myself. But if she doesn't stop, you know, if—

Father: (interrupts) But that's what you would be willing to do.

Son: Yeah. But we'll have to see if she stops it when I tell her.

Father: Okay. You'll do your part. Will you keep this agreement for at least one week? A good solid week?

Son: Okay. We'll see what happens.

As a result of this meeting, the son, with Jim's encouragement, kept to his promise. Tensions did ease between the siblings and peace was restored to the household.

2. Susan was a six-year-old with a severe hearing impairment. Her parents were very concerned because Susan would often leave her backyard play area and wander around the neighborhood (always returning by herself). Up till now, Susan's parents were dealing with the problem by watching her as much as possible.

Because they could not keep up constant surveillance, Susan would invariably wander off. Susan's parents used the requesting approach in a way suited to their needs. They decided to draw a picture of "Susan in the backyard" and asked Susan if she would promise to stay there when she was playing. When Susan nodded in agreement, they asked her to put her name on the picture (to signify her agreement). An hour later, Susan went out to play and wandered away. After locating her, they returned her to the house, brought out the picture, and, without anger, erased her name. After explaining to Susan that her name was erased because she did not keep the agreement, they once again asked Susan if she wanted to put her name back on the picture. Susan said no! Her parents were not sure why she did this, but respected her answer. They let her outside again and remained with her to ensure her staying in the yard. The next day, they repeated the *requesting* procedure. This time it went well. Over the course of the week, there were two more incidents in which Susan wandered off. Each time Susan decided to put her name back on the picture and kept her promise. The following week, no further incidents occurred.

Comments

Allowing your child to make an offer to change her behavior is an excellent first plan or a valuable corrective if you have previously been trying too hard to make the behavior change all by yourself. It is best suited for adolescents, but can easily be done with children as young as five years old by making a specific proposal (e.g., making your own bed) and asking for agreement. No matter how serious the behavior in question and how belligerent your child is about it, always consider *requesting* as an option.

Option 2: Reminding

Although you have explained your reasons until you're blue in the face, your child may continue to behave in an unacceptable manner. One plan to consider it to remind your child *on a daily basis* what behavior is acceptable and what is not (until change occurs). Through daily restatements of rules and expectations, your child learns that you will persist with your requests regardless of his attempts to change your mind. Often it is not necessary to do anything else to help a child change his behavior.

What to Do

There are three key elements in using *reminding* as an option:

1. Select a specific behavior you'd like to change.

2. Communicate your expectation about this behavior on some fixed schedule; don't wait for infractions to occur.

3. Resolve that you will not discuss your feelings about your child's lack of cooperation with her, *nor* will you respond to her objections, until you've given the plan at least one week.

You can state your expectation verbally or to older children in writing. If you verbalize your request, keep your remarks straightforward, brief, and simple. For example, a young child can be told upon entering a playroom, "I am counting on you to pick up the toys you use when you are finished playing," or, upon arriving at the dinner table, "Your job is to use your fork to pick up your food." An older child can be reminded when he comes home from school, "The rule is, only one hour of TV this afternoon," or, during dinner, "Ask for help if you don't understand your homework." If you feel like a nag, try leaving written messages about rules and regulations. Short notes to an older child are clear, effective methods of communication and avoid misunderstandings between you both. "KEEP THE DOOR CLOSED"; "REMINDER: YOUR ROOM MUST BE CLEANED UP TONIGHT." If you don't get results, it is always possible to take immediate, short-term action (e.g., put toys away or unplug the TV for the remainder of the day) and then return the next day to merely *reminding* your child in advance of trouble.

Case Examples

1. Millie, a single parent, was very upset because since her divorce six months before, her eight-year-old daughter Ann had gained fifteen pounds. Feeling very guilty over the impact of the divorce on Ann, Millie was reluctant to do anything about the weight gain, preferring instead, to ignore it. Upon learning about the ten basic options, Millie chose *reminding*. She wrote down a

list of food restrictions for Ann and presented it. Explaining that there would be no anger or punishment, Millie told Ann that she would instead simply go over the list *every day* before breakfast and dinner. The plan worked. After a week of *reminding,* Millie announced to her daughter that she was trusted to handle herself around food. Reassured by her mother's quiet, but steady persistence and then inspired by her mother's faith in her, the daughter lost five pounds over the next month. The problem of overeating did not occur again.

2. Joe was a moody fifteen-year-old who rarely communicated with his parents. He sat silently through meals and retreated behind closed doors in his bedroom at other times. His parents were extremely concerned by this behavior and launched into long discourses whenever they could with Joe as to why communication was so important. Much of what they had to say was quite eloquent, but Joe usually warded off his parents with the comments, "Don't worry, I'm all right. Leave me alone." After long thought, Joe's parents developed an interesting *reminding* plan. They sat down with Joe and told him that, no matter how difficult it was for him, he was expected to communicate one thing on his own initiative every day. To remind him, before his parents went to bed, they left a message on his bedroom door each night, saying "Communicate." Instead of the same sign each night, Joe's parents varied the signs, using different colors and lettering. They did nothing else. It took until the third day for Joe to initiate communication (his first attempt was to report that he got a B on a science test). Thereafter, he slowly initiated more and more. Joe's parents listened well and responded briefly (no more long discourses). After two weeks of signs, Joe asked his parents to stop and they agreed. Communication, thereafter, greatly improved.

Comments

Reminding is a slow but steady method. Its success depends on systematic, quiet repetition. Some parents resist using this option by claiming: "My child *should* know what he's supposed to do." Don't fall into this trap. Children often benefit from *reminding* as long as parents don't become nags in the process. *Reminding* can be used for all ages, but it will not bring dramatic results with tots who are out of control or with teenagers who really want to test your limits. It is highly recommended for parents who discuss, implore, and plead a lot or who always wait for trouble to brew before reacting. It can be combined easily with other plans.

Option 3: Monitoring

Monitoring is a plan to consider when close supervision is indicated and can be arranged. It involves staying with a child to make sure your wishes are fulfilled or making frequent checks on her behavior. *Monitoring* should not be confused with spying; your child ought to know that her behavior is being monitored. Otherwise the purpose of *monitoring*—to act as external control for your child—is defeated.

What to Do

Select a problem behavior that might benefit from close supervision. Choose whether your plan will involve "checking in" or actually remaining physically present for a longer period of time. If you prefer to make frequent checks, decide upon a schedule and keep to it as much as you can. For example, a child can be monitored every fifteen minutes for a one- to two-hour period to determine whether he is doing homework or cleaning his room. When you come to the room, briefly compliment positive behavior or firmly request a return to what is expected. If you wish to remain a longer time, stay close to your child and physically intervene if necessary. For example, a parent might decide to spend a half hour every day (perhaps in three ten-minute sessions) shadowing an acting-out preschooler, making sure that no property is destroyed during that time, or baby brother or sister isn't hurt. Gradually reduce but do not eliminate the amount of time you spend monitoring a child's behavior over a one- to two-week period. Be careful to avoid enticing a child to defy you (by keeping too much distance or by setting up a dare with your eyes). Try instead to communicate that you expect the child to act the way you want. Before launching a *monitoring* plan, inform your child (six years or older) of your intentions in a respectful, matter-of-fact way: "I am going to check on you a lot during the next week to make sure you are (identify desired behavior). This is not a punishment. I want you to get better about (behavior)."

When dealing with a teenager, inject a little humor into the encounter so that she preserves some dignity. Above all, avoid criticism and put-downs.

Case Examples

1. George, a sixteen-year-old, had been caught in school with marijuana. When his heretofore easygoing parents confronted him about the matter, George promised not to do it again. Two weeks later, a similar report came from school. His parents, more concerned this time, brought George to a counselor. Again, George promised not to be involved with marijuana. When it happened a third time, George's parents decided to put a *monitoring* plan into effect. They explained to George that they were going to do everything possible to keep him away from pot. This included searching his room every day and searching him before he went to school. Also planned was a surveillance of George to and from school and frequent checks by teachers and school administrators on his movements between classes. Naturally, George objected to this invasion of his privacy. His parents responded: "We still are going to do everything we can to keep you away from this stuff." George complained bitterly and told his parents that they were treating him like a child. He could take care of the matter without their supervision. Nonetheless, the *monitoring* went on for two weeks. George got the message. No further incidents occurred.

2. Jill, a three-year-old with marked developmental delays, was a terror around the early intervention program she attended three times weekly with her mother. Every toy on every shelf would be pulled down and thrown. Jill was able to clear a whole bookcase in ten seconds if left unsupervised. Both staff and her mother would do what they could to stop her from going to the toys. To change tactics, a decision was made to bring Jill to a bookcase of toys for five-minute sessions, six times a morning. During those sessions, her movements were closely monitored and corrected. Often it was necessary to stop her ten times a minute from destructively interacting with the toys. Yet she was allowed to continue playing, with an adult doing everything possible to control her. To counteract fatigue, a team of adults took turns in three five-minute sessions. After one week of

constant supervision there was noticeable improvement. By the next week, Jill was able to play through most of the five-minute sessions without correction. By the third week, she was allowed longer time periods with the toys and required considerably less supervision.

Comments

Monitoring can take a lot of time and effort. It is worthwhile whenever a child needs a good dosage of external control, but it should not be done if you can't expend the energy. It is particularly recommended for a parent who always tries one-shot solutions or who looks for shortcuts to change persistent problems. It is also indicated if you feel a great deal of despair about your child's ability to change her behavior. *Monitoring* can be extended outside the home by asking others to report on your child's behavior. Daily reports from a teacher can be particularly helpful.

Option 4: Ignoring

Ignoring is a plan to discourage negative behaviors by not responding to them and attending instead to behaviors you want to encourage.

What to Do

Many parents make the mistake of ignoring misbehavior once in a while and choosing other options at other times. This strategy tends to backfire because children sometimes see even punishment as adult attention. Ignoring a behavior must be planned. If there are two parents, both of you must decide together to ignore a behavior. When one parent is ignoring and the other is punishing, there is little hope that the behavior will stop. Any attention will encourage a child. Ignoring should be done calmly with no dramatics. If a child sees you upset as you are trying to ignore him, the plan will not be successful.

Case Examples

1. Kate and Steve had a three-year-old son, Sean, who stayed at a day-care center while both parents worked at a nearby office building. During the thirty-minute trip home from the center, they passed many fast-food restaurants. When Sean spotted

the first one, he'd ask for fries or ice cream, even though snacks were available in the car. As soon as his request was turned down, he'd tantrum without stop the rest of the trip. Once he even turned blue, almost passing out. Usually, Kate and Steve pulled off the road and begged Sean to stop the tantrums, promising to give him a treat when he got home. Kate and Steve were advised to give Sean a brief no and then totally ignore the tantrums during the rest of the trip. They were also instructed to give him undivided attention during the trip whenever he was not tantruming. The plan was very difficult for Kate and Steve to implement. The first day Kate caved in and gave attention to the tantrums, and the second day Steve followed suit. On the third day, they resolved to mutually ignore the tantrums, using the radio and whatever adult conversation they could muster to avoid paying attention. Confronted with the total lack of response from both parents, Sean lessened his tantrums so that by week's end they were a thing of the past.

2. Jennifer, a thirteen-year-old, used a lot of makeup, particularly eye shadow, much to her father's displeasure. He had been badgering Jennifer for months to stop, but Jennifer could always count on her mother to intervene on her behalf. Her mother kept telling her husband it was only a phase that Jennifer and all her friends were going through. Although dismayed by his wife's permissiveness, Jennifer's father persisted in admonishing his daughter. Meeting together with a counselor, Jennifer's parents agreed to the following plan. For one week, the father would make no comments about the makeup. Relieved of the burden of defending her daughter from her husband's badgering, Jennifer's mother was free to take a look at the situation on her own terms. During the week, the mother realized that she, too, was unhappy about the excessive makeup and negotiated some compromises with Jennifer. Father continued to stay out of the matter, and after a month Jennifer rarely put on makeup again.

Comments

Ignoring is an appropriate response to attention-bidding actions such as clowning, excessive dependence on adult help, protests, and tantrums.

When deciding to ignore a misbehavior, it is important to ask yourself the following questions:

- If the behavior is ignored, can tangible, harmful consequences occur before the behavior stops? You would not want to ignore a child who hits a sibling, but you could ignore a temper tantrum.

- Does the way you ignore communicate indifference or disapproval? Try to learn to live with the behavior that is upsetting you. You don't want to communicate disapproval, you want to communicate calm indifference.

- Is your attention important enough to the child that *ignoring* will make a difference? Your attention may not be enough of a reward. Children sometimes misbehave to get encouragement from their peers. If you decide that this is the case, choose another option.

Finally, ask yourself if you tend to overreact to the behavior you want to change. If the answer is yes, then *ignoring* may be for you because your overreaction could be reinforcing the child's misbehavior.

Option 5: Charting

A simple procedure for coping with your child's continuing resistance to your wishes is to keep a record of the number of infractions and share the results with the child. Without having to scream, nag, or communicate much at all, *charting* allows you to increase your child's awareness of how often he may be violating your rules. As a result, your child might possibly take some responsibility to improve his performance.

What to Do

Begin by selecting a target behavior you would like to change. Keep a record for one day of how many times your child does this negative behavior. Tell her the results and explain that you are tired of yelling all the time and would rather keep the same kind of record for the rest of the week. *Quietly* encourage her to improve (e.g., "Let's see if you can cut down on leaving things where they don't belong"), but be careful not to express too much eagerness or else your child will realize she now has the power to disappoint or upset you.

You may do just as well charting positive behaviors instead of negative ones. Keep your chart in a place where the child can see his progress in relative privacy (e.g., the child's bedroom). Use a sheet of paper with the target behavior specified in writing for older children (and pictorially for younger ones), the days of the week, and spaces for marks entered when infractions occur. As a variation, you can deposit pennies or paper clips in a glass jar. If you feel that an actual counting of infractions is not helpful or possible, you can, instead, create a "needs improvement" sheet with a daily entry of "yes" or "no." If you feel that your child's progress is too slow after a week, you might consider adding rewards or penalties for promoting improvement.

Case Examples

1. Karen, a ten-year-old, would often disregard the first requests her mother made to do something. It usually took several more requests to get Karen to cooperate. Sometimes Karen's mother would get extremely angry in the process; other times she would back off and forget about the request entirely. Eventually, Karen's mother decided to sit down with Karen and discuss a *charting* plan.

> Mother: Karen, I don't think you realize how many times it takes to get you to do something.

> Karen: Well, you always act as if I have to stop everything to do what you want.

> Mother: I disagree, but let's not argue about it. What I'd like to do is keep a record this week of how many times you listen to me the first time I ask you to do something. Even if you say to me, "Can I do it in a few minutes?" I'll count that.

> Karen: Do I get something if I'm good?

> Mother: No, I'm not willing to reward you for this. I simply want you to work hard at increasing your record day by day.

>Karen: Mom, I think this is really stupid.

>Mother: It's okay if you feel that way. I can understand.
>But I'm still going to do it.

Because Karen's mother understood that *charting* can be effective whether or not the child likes it, she wasn't discouraged from using this option. Gradually Karen came to understand her mother's complaint and was proud that she improved. In return, her mother was less annoyed with Karen.

2. Nick was a five-year-old who was learning to do self-help skills such as dressing himself, brushing his teeth, and putting his comforter on his bed each morning. His parents had been monitoring his activity in this regard. Of course, whenever they failed to do so Nick did not remember on his own. They decided to use *charting* for each of these areas. With regard to toothbrushing, for instance, they would say, "Nick, sometimes you brush your teeth and some days you forget." Nick would respond, "Most of the time I remember."

>Parent: We don't think that's true. We think there are some mornings and some nights when you forget. And I'll tell you what we are going to do. We are going to put this chart in the bathroom. It says: Nick, did you brush your teeth? Then it has the days of the week. Let's hear you read them.

>Nick: Monday, Tuesday, Wednesday, Thursday, Friday, Saturday, and Sunday.

>Parent: Good. If you brush your teeth in the morning on a Monday (which is today), we'll put a check. If you remember to do it tonight, we'll put another check. Would you like to put the check marks?

>Nick: Yes!

>Parent: Let's see if you can do so well that there are checks every day.

Comments

Many parents assume that *charting* can work only if a child likes it. Although *charting* works better if the idea is agreeable to your child, you can go ahead with it even if she disapproves of the idea. Should your child try to argue that charting is unwarranted, invite her to do the charting. If your *charting* plan is labeled "silly" or "ridiculous," respond, "That may be your opinion, but I still want to try it." *Charting* can be done with children over four years of age. With a teenager, you should be especially careful to be discreet. You can also give her an informal verbal evaluation each day (in a calm, respectful manner) rather than use a written form. *Charting* is particularly recommended to parents who are overly talkative, tend to get upset easily, or get sidetracked by their children's protests.

Option 6: Rewarding

Rewarding is a plan to encourage positive behaviors by establishing tangible incentives for improvement. Parents often confuse rewarding with bribery. A bribe entices a child to stop negative behavior and a reward promotes new, positive behaviors to replace negative ones. Bribery is often what adults resort to when they are frantic. By contrast, *rewarding* is a careful plan to promote expectations that a child finds difficult, anxiety-provoking, or unappealing. The parent who uses *rewarding* as a plan is fully "in charge."

What to Do

Generally speaking, it is desirable to inform a child (over four years old) about your plan to encourage him to earn a reward. With children under four, it is usually better to "catch them" doing the positive behavior (e.g., informing you when they need to be brought to the toilet) and then immediately provide a reward. Discussion with older children should cover what an incentive system is. Explain that some things people need to learn to do on a regular basis may not seem very rewarding in and of themselves (e.g., cleaning a room, doing homework, etc.). Children, like adults, sometimes need incentives to do these things. Once they are being done regularly, children learn to value these things and rewards are no longer needed. Then, share your plan of what will happen, for what the reward is to be given, and *for how long*. This last part is important because eventually you will want to stop the plan and explain to the child that an incentive is no longer needed.

While money is a good incentive, there are lots of things that are rewarding to children. The following list contains some possibilities.

Early Childhood

A child can earn dessert by eating her main course.

A child can have extra playtime for behaving well with other children.

A child can help cook dinner if he picks up the toys.

A child earns a story if she goes to bed without complaint.

A child earns a nickel for dressing quickly in the morning.

A child earns a treat for behaving well in a store.

A child earns a small toy for behaving well during a car ride.

(Note that with young children the reward is given right away. Young children have difficulty waiting for rewards.)

Middle Childhood

A child earns points for doing household chores. The points can be redeemed for money, TV time, dinner out, etc.

A child earns his allowance for chores done.

A child earns TV time for homework completed.

A child who comes home from school on time for five days earns the right to have a friend sleep over on a weekend night.

A child earns a rented video for a week without junk food.

A child earns chips for practicing the piano. The chips are reimbursable for a desired game, sweater, or record.

Adolescence

A teenager earns car privileges for coming in on time.

A teenager earns clothes for bringing up a poor grade.

A teenager earns a party by doing extra, but needed, chores.

A teenager earns the right to take a part-time job by maintaining acceptable grades for one marking period.

A teenager earns an hour extension of curfew on the weekend by coming home on time during the week.

Case Examples

1. Gerald was a four-year-old boy who routinely came into his parents' bedroom during the middle of the night to sleep with them. Gerald's parents had been trying to ignore his presence but to no avail. The suggestion was made to buy a variety of toy cars and other small items Gerald liked and explain to him that he could select a toy for every night he remained in his bedroom. At first, the parents balked at this *rewarding* plan. They feared that Gerald would be difficult if he did not receive a toy after failing to stay in his room. Urged to give the plan a try, Gerald's parents withstood his tantrums when he was not successful and pleasantly rewarded him when he was. After three days, Gerald stayed in his room during the night for the remainder of the week. When the week was up, the parents simply told Gerald that he should stay in his room without the promise of toys. Gerald tested his parents for two nights and they considered returning to the rewarding plan. Instead, they decided to hold firm for the remainder of the week and Gerald never again came into their bedroom.

2. Beth, a fifteen-year-old, did not like to participate in family meals or attend other family events. Her mother Charlotte recognized Beth's separation from the family was normal for a teenager but Charlotte still felt that she had the right to expect some participation from Beth. Despite her pleas, however, Charlotte was unable to get much response. Deciding to give *rewarding* a try, Charlotte requested a short meeting in which she proposed to Beth an "exchange." For every night Beth was willing to participate in the family dinner, Charlotte promised to do Beth's daily chores. The exchange offer was good for one week. Beth was somewhat disarmed by the offer. Impressed by how serious her mother was about her membership in the family, Beth agreed. Things went so well that, after the week, Beth regularly came to dinner and even participated in some other family events.

Comments

Rewarding works best when you feel that things just haven't been going well at all or when you have been trying to deal with the problem in a variety of ways and, consequently, have been feeling inconsistent. A reward system focuses your (and your child's) attention on the positive. This calms down the parent and child. The decrease in frustration also alleviates parental fears that they will overreact or explode. *Rewarding* also provides needed consistency without laying the blame on the child or parents.

Option 7: Encouraging

Encouraging is a plan to promote positive behaviors by compliment-ing any actions that are steps toward the desired results. It differs from rewarding by using social reinforcers (expressions of appre-ciation, praise, attention, smiling, embraces) rather than tangible reinforcers (treats, privileges, etc.). So often, when a child is not doing what we hope for, the usual response is to bear down on the failures. Usually, if we look hard enough, we can catch posi-tive behaviors to compliment that, if nurtured, will bring about the overall result we are seeking.

What to Do

Identify a behavior you wish your child would improve upon. Notice and compliment even partial success or improvement. For younger children, *encouraging* helps to guide them through a learning sequence such as eating, toilet training, cleaning up toys, or dressing. In an example of learning to pour drinks, a parent might say: "Bring the pitcher right next to the glass. Good. Hold the pitcher with two hands. Great! Now pour a tiny bit to see if it will work. Yeah, it does. Good work. Okay, you can pour the juice in the glass to just before the top. Fine! Good for you." As you guide your child, avoid any criticism if a mistake occurs. Simply correct his actions and praise any level of success. With older children, *encouraging* helps to reduce resistance to undertaking new respon-sibilities or persisting with unattractive tasks (homework, chores, etc.). Instead of negative remarks, you make up your mind to remain positive about your child's efforts. For example, you might say to a child who makes an attempt to fold clothes with little success, "Thanks for trying to fold your shirts instead of rolling them up in a ball. I want to show you again how to fold your clothes so that you don't get any wrinkles." You might also consider *encouraging* to shape positive social behaviors such as friendly smiles (instead of frowns), improved communication, and relationship with siblings.

Case Examples

1. Debby, three years old, loved to bother her father whenever he was engaged in conversation with others. This was especially true if Dad was on the phone. He would become so angry when the interruptions occurred that he would wind up threatening to cancel Debby's favorite activity with Dad—bedtime stories. However, Dad's threats would never materialize, for he, too, was fond of reading and telling Debby stories. Debby's father did not think that an *encouraging* plan would make much sense in his circumstance because, as he explained, "there is nothing to encourage." As an experiment, therefore, he was counseled to praise Debby within seconds of his starting a conversation if she did not interrupt him. By continuing the praise (if warranted) after every minute of conversation, the father consistently reinforced Debby's willingness to wait. This simple (but frequent) encouragement worked wonders. Debby was willing to accept her father's conversations with a minimum of encouragement thereafter.

2. Jon, a fourteen-year-old, had a penchant for looking and dressing sloppily. His hair was long and messy, his shirttail was always sticking out, and his shoes were usually untied. Jon's parents constantly berated him for his slovenly appearance with virtually no success. Even on important occasions, Jon would look as if he had slept in his clothes all night. To start off an *encouraging* plan, Jon's parents decided to sit down with him and tell him, "We really want you to make an effort to improve your appearance. You're a good-looking kid and we want to see your good looks. For this week, however, instead of complaining about your appearance, we will compliment it whenever you do a little to improve." True to their word, Jon's parents complimented any small improvement. They were careful not to sound insincere. They also kept their praise low-key and to the point. During the week, some improvement occurred but not enough to assume that any significant change would occur. So Jon's parents kept to the plan for a second week. Their quiet willingness to be encouraging rather than critical finally was successful. Jon began to tuck in his shirt, comb his hair, and the like. Although he was no fashion plate, his appearance certainly improved.

Comments

Parents often defeat their own proposes by giving children gushy or exaggerated praise. Children, like adults, do not believe overly effusive compliments. They may also feel manipulated and resist learning new skills. Straightforward, no-fuss messages produce the best results: "Good job"; "That was better"; "Nice going." *Encouraging* is especially recommended to parents who find themselves getting nowhere with criticism or believe that their child is very discouraged about her abilities.

Option 8: Teaching

Teaching is often not thought of as a discipline strategy despite the fact that the Latin derivative of the word *discipline* means "teach." Nonetheless, literally teaching a child what is expected is often helpful. *Teaching* involves helping a child learn both how to do something and to understand its purpose. An educational approach to a problem often enlists a child's cooperation and is a major option in helping to change behavior.

What to Do

Examine the problem behavior you have selected and ask yourself whether your child has (1) the skill to make the change and (2) an understanding of why the current behavior is problematic. If the skill needs to be taught, first identify all the parts of the skill. Be sure to analyze exactly what your child needs to perform the skill. Next, decide on a teaching strategy. Consider the use of visual aids, demonstration, drill, role-playing, quizzes, directed discussion, reading, games, and any other teaching technique you feel might work. The same procedure holds true for the understanding side of the problem. If you think there is a possibility you can help your child appreciate the meaning of his behavior, identify all the aspects of the problem and select an appropriate teaching strategy. It is often difficult to explain something to a child. Try to compare what you are teaching to something your child readily understands. For example, if you are trying to teach a young child not to eat in the living room, you could tell the child, "You know that people don't sleep in a kitchen. People also don't eat in the living room."

Case Examples

1. Vickie decided that her ten-year-old son's aversion to vegetables might benefit from a *teaching* approach. For several years, Vickie had tried to force the issue. At first, her son had to eat his vegetables (even some of them) if he wanted any dessert. After years of missed desserts, she took to refusing to let him leave the table until he choked down the vegetables. Key to the *teaching* plan was to give it plenty of time. Vickie explained to her son that he did not have to eat vegetables, but he did have to try to understand their value. Over the course of a month, Vickie held several "lessons" on the virtues of vegetables. To make the lessons fun, she dug up interesting facts about various vegetables. Vickie also taught her son how to peel and cook vegetables. Trips to the supermarket included lessons on the seasonal fluctuations in price and quality of certain vegetables. To top off the "program," vegetables were jointly planted in the garden. When the month was over, Vickie asked her son if he wanted to try a stir-fry vegetable recipe they would mutually prepare. Her son insisted that the vegetables had to be shredded and combined with lo mein noodles. With these provisions, the meal was a success and the son was open to trying vegetables in different forms. Vickie's son is now in college and eats vegetarian!

2. Laurie had always been a very shy child. Wisely, her parents accepted her shyness and never criticized her for it. Now that Laurie was seven, however, her parents realized that she needed some guidance in dealing with certain social situations. They began with the problem of meeting new people. Laurie's parents wrote down the skills that Laurie needed: Look at the person who is addressing you, answer questions simply and directly, and remain in the person's presence until he is finished. Then they role-played a scene for Laurie to demonstrate the skills and practiced the scene with her. At first, Laurie resisted but her parents were quietly determined to continue. Practice sessions occurred each night for a week. Laurie's parents maintained an encouraging but persistent approach throughout. The following week, a large family wedding occurred. Laurie was prompted how to handle situations that might arise. In fact, she handled

them beautifully. As a result, Laurie's self-esteem increased, and, although not a social butterfly, she now is adequate in social situations.

Comments

Your teaching style is critical to the success of this approach. Try to be warm, creative, and persistent. If you meet resistance, don't continue unless you can remain calm and confident. It is better to drop the "lesson" and continue on another occasion. This approach demands a lot from you. Although it requires preparation and patience, it can be a very powerful approach to helping your child.

Option 9: Backing Off

Some children delight in giving parents a hard time. It feeds a false sense of self-worth: I am worthwhile because I can manipulate my parents. In this instance, it is especially appropriate to consider *backing off.* The idea behind *backing off* is to shift gears in the way you help a child change her behavior. Instead of pressing your usual demands and getting defiance, you temporarily give up your expectations and thereby leave your child with a parent who can't be pushed around. Once accomplished, a child may be willing to change her own behavior.

What to Do

There are two basic ways to back off:

1. "The choice is yours," you announce to your child, explaining that for a while you will stop demanding a particular change in behavior. Tell the child that you are tired of nagging, screaming, and the like and are taking a rest. The choice of whether any change occurs is left up to the child.

   Example
   Parent: "I'm tired of getting after you about the way you treat your sister. I'm going to leave the matter in your hands for a while. You're old enough to figure out yourself whether you should treat your sister any differently."

2. "You can't": You share with your child the observation that he has a lot of difficulty doing what you expect and therefore you

are going to give up your expectation for a while and accept your child's limitations.

Example
Parent: "You have a lot of trouble remembering to use a napkin to wipe your hands. It would be easier if we go back to a bib."

Generally speaking, "the choice is yours" approach is best suited for children over six while the "you can't" tactic can be used easily with younger children. Both strategies work best when your goal is to show your child, in a subtle way, that he has the power to choose a different course of action. Therefore, do not delight in outwitting your child by these tactics. Remain matter-of-fact and honest. Give your child a reasonable amount of time to act maturely on his own. If no change occurs after one or two weeks, it is always possible to renew your active efforts to change behavior.

Case Examples

1. Ellen and Bob were fond of taking long walks on the weekend. Their five-year-old daughter Nancy always wanted to accompany them, but invariably asked to be carried along the way. Usually Ellen and Bob responded with annoyance to this request and threatened Nancy that they would not take her along for walks again. Nancy got her way, however, after a lot of whining and sit-down strikes. Upon learning about *backing off*, Ellen and Bob decided to give it a try. Before their next walk, they sat down with Nancy and explained to her, "You know, Nancy, you really do get tired walking by yourself. Whenever you get tired, tell us and we'll carry you." This message was delivered matter-of-factly, with no hint of being derogatory. As they walked, Ellen and Bob said frequently, "Tell us if you're tired." As they had hoped, Nancy was almost defiant in proclaiming, "No, I can make it home." And she did. Before future walks, Ellen and Bob repeated the same strategy and enjoyed continued success.

2. Sal and Fran were very concerned over their daughter Lisa's academic performance during the beginning of her junior year in high school. Considering upcoming college applications, it was no time, they felt, to permit their daughter's grades to suffer.

As a result, they lectured, nagged, supervised, threatened, and scolded Lisa about her schoolwork. Yet most of the time, Lisa resisted and did the minimum. Her grades began to fall below her usual performance. Sal and Fran were beside themselves with anger, on the one hand, and uncertainty, on the other. When *backing off* was first explained to them, they laughed it off. But when another week passed by in which their customary efforts failed, Sal and Fran decided to give it a brief but sincere try. They requested a short meeting with Lisa and began by saying, "Lisa, we've been on you about your schoolwork a whole lot this year, and we're not sure we want to do that anymore. You're getting older and we want this to be your responsibility. So we sat down and thought about it and decided that it was time for us to stop getting on you about this. For at least the next week, we're not going to say anything about your schoolwork." Almost immediately, Lisa responded, "Okay!" Startled, Lisa's father asked, "You're sure now?" Lisa replied, "Yeah. When you hassle me, it makes me not want to do it. It gets on my nerves." "Well, maybe that's the problem!" retorted Sal. "I don't know, but we think it should be up to you for the next two weeks." Indeed, Lisa did take growing responsibility for her schoolwork and her parents' scolding turned to admiration. In doing the opposite of what Lisa expected, it was as if Sal and Fran helped Lisa to see through the illusion she held that stubborn resistance was her only avenue of self-determination. Now Lisa discovered she had the power to assert herself positively rather than negatively.

Comments

Backing off tactics are highly experimental. Their chance of working depends so much on the child's response that it would be foolhardy to guarantee success. Nonetheless, *backing off* should definitely be considered by parents who have been in constant power struggles with their children. Try it initially in a situation that involves a relatively minor conflict and see how it feels and works.

Option 10: Penalizing

Penalizing is a plan to deter the reoccurrence of unacceptable behavior. Typically, it involves the loss of a privilege or physical restrictions. It is one of the most widely but ineffectively used plans parents adopt when coping with misbehavior. All too frequently, penalties are a way parents express anger at their children. To really help children change their behavior, penalties are effective when they focus on the misdeed instead of the doer.

What to Do

Identify a negative behavior that you don't want your child to repeat. Avoid behaviors for which immediate and total compliance is not expected. If you are content with gradual improvement, it would be better to use some of the other options. Next, decide what consequence would be effective as a deterrent. Make sure that your parenting partner will support this penalty. Present the penalty to your child and be sure to specify the behavior for which it is meant. It is helpful to think of yourself as a sort of umpire or referee who knows that she has the power to penalize and who usually turns a deaf ear to complaints of unfairness. For example, parents might say to a child who is routinely late for school, "From now on we are instituting a new policy. If you are not downstairs for breakfast, ready for school by 7:15, you will go to bed thirty minutes earlier that evening." A list of sample penalties follows.

Early Childhood

A child is held tightly for one minute for having a temper tantrum.

A child's toys are put out of sight for one day when they are left on the floor.

A child is removed from the dinner table for throwing food.

A child must sit quietly for three minutes in a "time-out" chair each time he is racing recklessly in the living room.

A child is removed from play for hitting another child.

(Note that most of the penalties are either physical or involve removal from the activity. These actions should be accompanied by a simple explanation such as "people are not for hitting.")

Middle Childhood

A child who doesn't complete her homework loses TV privileges for the next day.

A child loses a percentage of his allowance for undone chores.

A child is sent to his room when returning from a shopping trip for causing a disruption.

A child who is riding her bike dangerously loses bike privileges for a week.

A child who comes home two hours late is assigned two hours of work around the house.

Adolescence

A teenager who violates curfew is grounded for one week (with no visitors).

A teenager who constantly ties up the phone loses phone privileges for each day that the behavior continues.

If a teenager skips school, the school is called to report that he was AWOL.

A teenager who curses and strikes a parent is sent for two days to a relative.

If chores are not done, refuse to do some of the things you do for your teenager until the situation changes.

Case Examples

1. Gary was a spirited, competitive eight-year-old. His major problem was peer relationships. He controlled play activity, rarely sharing or involving others, trying to win at all costs. Whenever they witnessed this behavior, Gary's parents were quite upset with him, but if they confronted Gary about his competitiveness, he would place the blame on the other kids with whom he was playing. In response, Gary's parents would ground him from time to time to try to "get through to him." At first, Gary would protest and then wind up promising to

include other peers to end the grounding. He rarely kept his promises. When Gary's parents learned about the ten basic options, they considered using an alternative to *penalizing* but then realized that a different, perhaps more creative penalty than grounding might be tried. The penalty they decided upon was a long "walk and talk" with a parent. When either parent witnessed or received a report about Gary's competitive behavior, they would take a thirty-minute walk with him during which his behavior was discussed. Typically, Gary would do almost anything to get out of confrontations with a parent, so he disliked these "walk and talks." Nonetheless, they were successful. Besides acting as a deterrent, the "walk and talks" also were an effective means of helping Gary to gain greater awareness of and control over his competitive behavior.

2. Sammy was an overactive two-and-a-half-year-old who would throw objects, hit and bite people, and tantrum at will. His parents were able to control him for only short periods of time, usually by spanking him. When they heard about the technique of "time-out," they immediately dismissed its appropriateness for Sammy. However, they were urged to give it a try. The first problem they incurred was keeping Sammy in a "time-out" chair. They realized it would be necessary to hold him in a chair for a one-minute time-out. Although Sammy would kick and fuss, one parent was able to restrain him. Despite his protests, he was praised for "doing time-out well" when the minute was up. The next question to arise was how frequently to use time-out. Sammy could use it sometimes more than ten times an hour! The decision was made to select three one-hour periods a day in which time-out would be utilized as frequently as necessary. During other times of the day, Sammy's parents would try to monitor his behavior as much as possible, using spankings only when absolutely necessary. The final practical problem was where to place a time-out chair. Sammy's mother found it impractical to use the same place as she moved around the house doing the cleaning, cooking, or other chores. The suggestion was made to utilize any convenient site including the steps to the second floor and the kitchen table. By consistently using time-out throughout early childhood, Sammy's parents were able to teach Sammy self-control. Sammy was actually reassured by

time-out and enjoyed the praise he received for doing it well. At times, he even went to time-out on his own initiative.

Comments

Parents often get into trouble by penalizing spontaneously. One mother I knew would ground her son for a week or two for every infraction. The time mounted up until the boy felt there was no hope for parole before the age of twenty-one! Instead of trying to behave, he got worse. Another trap some parents fall into is to impose penalties that punish them as much, if not more, than the child (e.g., setting up a penalty that requires your constant supervision). You're more likely to follow through on a penalty if it can be supervised easily. Better yet, consider "going on strike," that is, refusing to do something for your child that is normally expected (e.g., chauffeuring, cooking, packing a school lunch, etc.). It is important to warn your child ahead of time about the penalty in a calm moment. Then penalizing is not an act of anger; it is a method of behavior management. Finally, it is imperative to remember that penalties must be followed by reinforcement of positive behavior for change to occur.

DEVELOPING YOUR PLAN

Now that you have read about the options open to you, you are ready to develop your own plan of action. Here are five steps to take at this point.

1. With the behavior you chose on page 59 in mind, list all the things you have done up till now that have *not* been successful in changing the situation. Look over the list and compare it to the ten basic options for changing children's behavior.

2. Write down *all* the options that would represent a different approach than you have previously taken. Include an approach that you have tried but have not applied consistently enough to rule out its effectiveness.

3. Select one or two options from Step 2 with which you are willing to experiment seriously. In your selection, don't be afraid to take a risk with an option you would normally avoid. Remember that your capacity to change helps your child's ability to change.

In addition, you should review the general reasons discussed in Chapter 2 (see pages 25-27) that your children may be exhibiting the problem behavior. The reasons you identify will help you select an appropriate option.

4. To work out the details of your selected option, reread the instructions, case examples, and comments about that option in this chapter. Give it some thought and include other adults in your planning. The more confident you are about the plan and the more support you have behind you, the more likely you will succeed. If you are especially concerned about the lack of support or interference by others, read the next chapter before embarking on your plan.

5. Remember that after one to two weeks on the initial plan, you can switch to a different option if you are not successful. GOOD LUCK!

Questions and Answers

1. *You urge parents to avoid trying to change a child's attitude. Aren't attitudes more important than behaviors?*

   Attitudes are usually labels we give to explain why children behave the way they do, such as "he's lazy" or "she's sensitive." They are often not the root of the problem but a way to help us shift blame or excuse our inability to change things. When children are helped to behave in positive ways, their view of themselves improves and that's what really changes their "attitude."

2. *I've tried all your ideas and my child still is impossible. Why?*

   Probably, the problem has been that you have tried everything rather than settling on one approach and giving it a serious try (at least one week) before you switch to another.

3. *I would feel uncomfortable doing many of the ten basic options. They seem somewhat artificial to me. Do other parents feel that way?*

   Yes, some do, probably because they have utilized the same approach over and over again. As I have said, parents are sometimes as much of a discipline problem as are our children.

We expect children to change their ways but we don't change ours. The ten options represent most of the major techniques found in parenting books. Any other method, in and of itself, may be effective or ineffective. The important thing is for parents to have alternatives to the way they have approached the problem they are facing with their child.

4. *Is there any significance that penalizing is listed last? Is it the last resort?*

No. Sometimes it ought to be tried first. There is no significance to the order in which the ten basic options are listed.

5. *Then how do you choose which of the ten options is best for you?*

As I have said, it often makes little difference what new plan you undertake. For example, parents who have been punitive might switch to rewards; parents who have always tried to discuss things with their children might try ignoring. There are parents who feel that some options are better bets for different age children. Requesting works well with teenagers and charting often does the trick with younger children. Just don't rule out anything. Charting could serve parents of teenagers well and requesting can be done in a simple way with young children. All of the options can be applied to practically every child with whom there is some communication. Some options, such as ignoring, rewarding, penalizing, and monitoring, may be used even with nonverbal children.

6

Step 4:
Obtain Support
from Other Adults

Parenting a difficult child is made easier when there is ongoing support of other adults who live with or care for your child. For one thing, you'll feel less guilty about ignoring your child's temper tantrums or punishing him for failing to come home on time if you know another adult is behind you. For another, you'll feel better able to give your child loving attention if you know another adult is able to take over for you when you run out of patience.

Few parents, whether married or single, can expect to obtain this much needed support easily. Unfortunately, there are many obstacles to adults' working together as a cooperative "team." Many adults simply don't talk with each other about the children in their mutual charge because they fear that such decisions might cause uneasiness or even start a fight. Others do just the opposite. They use discussions about children as a way to express anger that is really aimed at each other. Finally, the children themselves are obstacles, playing one parent against the other, a teacher against a parent, etc.

Overcoming these obstacles, however, is important for any team of adults who want to keep their children's best interests in mind. Nothing can be more harmful to children than the knowledge that the adults in charge of them are in deep conflict with each other. The conflicts between the adults usually serve to confuse children. They get very different messages from each adult.

Of course, some difference of opinion between adults is normal and may even be good for the children. A "team" spirit between the adults is really the important thing, not perfect agreement or a rigid "united front." A team approach is simply a strong mutual commitment to do three things:

1. **Support:** Provide emotional support to each other.

2. **Feedback:** Give constructive criticism to each other.

3. **Planning:** Plan together how to deal with persistent problems or major issues.

Providing emotional support is basic to any team approach. You as well as your "teammate" need to count on someone else to help out, listen to your feelings, and appreciate your efforts.

Feedback is the constructive evaluation of your strengths and weaknesses as a parent. It includes advice on how to avoid the difficulties you fall prey to with your child. The feedback and advice does not have to be accepted for a team approach to work, but it does need to be heard (hopefully, not in front of your child).

Planning is a joint commitment to discuss rules, expectations, and discipline strategies for specific problem behaviors. Sometimes this planning can be done in anticipation of a problem, such as the return of your child to school after a vacation. Other times this planning is in response to an ongoing problem similar to the many considered in the previous chapter.

Many parents I know feel that they don't receive all the support, feedback, and planning help they desire. But before you blame the other adults who also care for your child, consider your own behavior first. How willing have you been to include others in the parenting of your child? Because you are the person reading this book, chances are that you consider yourself more interested, better informed, and more capable of helping your child than someone else. But remember: If you are truly confident, you can open yourself to the involvement of others. And what if those "others" don't want to be involved? *Do what you can to include them.* Your child will be the winner if you do.

HOW PARENTS DISQUALIFY EACH OTHER

If you share parenting duties with a spouse, relative, or hired child caretaker, there may be ways in which you are limiting your effectiveness as a team. I call these ways "disqualifers."

1. Allowing Others to Parent Your Children

One of the surest ways for parents, especially single parents, to be disqualified as the major source of influence in their children's lives is to allow an inappropriate person to perform a parenting role in the family. The most common mistake is to permit an older child to have a kind of parental status in the family by giving this child the responsibility of extensive child care of younger siblings or letting this child discipline them. Another pattern is to permit a relative, often a grandparent, to interfere with the raising of your children in major ways when the involvement of this relative is unnecessary. Parents have a right to be firm with relatives about their roles. Remember that you as the parent decide what is best for your children.

2. Keeping a Rigid Role Division

A rigid role division in a team means that one adult specializes in certain parenting functions and the other adult specializes in other functions. For example, one adult may do most of the disciplining and the other adult may do most of the caring—giving support, understanding, etc. When this occurs, both adults limit their lives as complete human beings, capable of being both in charge and involved.

3. Acting Impulsively

One or both adults can develop a pattern of acting too quickly and too independently when problems occur with children. By failing to check with one another, one part of the team does not know what the other is doing. Also, one adult's impulsive actions may preclude or rule out an excellent solution coming from the other adult.

4. Not Standing on Your Own Two Feet

A team approach, strangely enough, is severely limited when adults develop too much reliance on assisting each other. Neither adult will appear confident to a child if both must always confer with each other about a child's every request or attempt together to handle a problem requiring only one adult (e.g., taking a child to bed).

5. Directly Interfering with the Other Adult

Whenever one adult interferes with the actions of the other, the possibility of undermining that adult's effectiveness increases. This interference can occur when one adult is openly criticized or blatantly contradicted by the other in a conflict situation with a child. It also takes place when adults compete with each other for a child's approval and love.

GUIDELINES FOR TEAM PARENTING

I have developed five guidelines for working as a team to make family life harmonious. Talk over these guidelines and figure out how you can make a commitment to them.

1. Set aside a special time every week to talk over your children's problems and unsatisfactory behavior. Stick to the schedule and choose your strategies for solving problems or disciplining together.

2. If you want to try a new approach to dealing with your children's problems, ask each other for support or, at the very least, a policy of noninterference.

3. Don't cop out when you have to make a decision alone by saying, "We'll have to wait till your (other adult) comes home" or when a discipline problem needs immediate attention. The adult who is there at the time should handle the matter.

4. In a hassle with a child, avoid using the other adult as a physical or psychological backup (unless you are clearly overpowered) and don't butt in when the other adult is in the middle of a fight with the child or smooth things over afterwards. Let the other adult handle the conflict and do the same for yourself.

5. Resolve differences of opinion in raising your child in private, not in front of the child. And when expressing your gripes, be constructive and stick to the issues.

In following these guidelines, two special issues warrant comment. How can adults resolve their differences when they really disagree with each other? What do you do when a child comes to you seeking your support because of the negative actions of the other adult?

A team approach does not mean a bunch of watered-down compromises. Instead, one adult may be willing to back down temporarily because his views are not as strongly held as the other adult's. Also, some rules for children may apply only in the presence of one adult. A third possibility is to learn to make exchanges. You agree to an issue important to the other adult if he will go along on a different issue important to you. As a last resort, you might flip a coin. *I am convinced that adults working together as a team is often more important than what the team actually decides to do to resolve the behavior problems of the children.*

When a child seeks one adult's support against the other, there is little reason to give it. It's usually better to insist that the child work out her conflict directly with the other adult. If this arrangement is not feasible, it may work out to offer to discuss the child's feelings with the other adult, being careful not to promise to take the child's side. Only when the actions of one adult are dangerous to a child's emotional or physical well-being should another adult advocate for the child.

AN ILLUSTRATION OF TEAM PARENTING

When their children are being difficult, parents all too often get so frustrated that they wind up being difficult with each other as well. Consider, for example, two parents who have just come from a restaurant in which their young child has been very difficult. Notice how at first they argue and blame each other for what happened. However, they soon realize that a team approach to parenting is needed.

Mother: My head is aching. I just want to tell you this. I never want to eat in a restaurant with Patrick again.

Father: Oh, come on, Eileen!

Mother: No, I've had it. I cannot—

Father: (interrupts) There you go again. Why should we let Patrick dictate whether we go to a restaurant or not?

Mother: I'm not going to sit there and be embarrassed by this every time.

Father: It's your fault that every time Patrick acts up you pick him up and entertain him. You walk around the restaurant, even visiting the kitchen sometimes! I mean, it's ridiculous. I tell him to sit in his seat and just wait until his food comes.

Mother: But, honey, I just get so embarrassed when I see you screaming at Patrick in the restaurant. I just don't like people to stare at us.

Father: Why don't you tell Patrick to settle down?

Mother: If I walk around with him, at least it gives him something to do. At least he's occupied and he's not running all around . . . I think we should just give it up. We just won't go out for a while.

Father: Eileen! There must be something we can do about this.

Mother: It's just not worth it.

Father: Hold it. Maybe there is something we can agree on. You don't like the way I do things and I don't like the way you do things. Maybe there's something different we can agree about.

Mother: If you have something that will work, I'll listen. Okay?

Father: I'll tell you what. Instead of your being the one who marches Patrick around when he acts up, I'll take him out to the car and we'll sit there until the food comes to the table.

Mother: Oh terrific, so I have to sit there in the restaurant by myself. There's no sense in going out if I have to do that!

Father: But it will work!

Mother: Hold on a second. Do you think he's old enough to receive a punishment when he gets home if he's bad in the restaurant? Maybe if there's something—

Father: Now you're talking. We'll tell Patrick beforehand that if he acts up in the restaurant when he gets home he'll have to go right to bed.

Mother: Yeah, one night doing that might do it. He can't watch any TV. It will be right to bed.

Father: What do *we* do in the meantime in the restaurant when he's fussing? Can I take him out to the car?

Mother: I just don't want to sit there by myself. Can you tell him something before he's acting up? What are you going to tell him in advance?

Father: What are *we* going to tell him? Why does it have to be me?

Mother: You're right. We have to tell him that we want him to sit in his seat quietly until the food comes. And if he doesn't do that, we tell him that he has one more chance. Either he's quiet or he goes to bed as soon as we get home.

Father: Okay. Let's give it a whirl.

As you read the outcome of this team discussion, you may not feel that this couple's plan will work. There certainly are other alternatives they might consider. The important thing at the moment, though, is that they are working together.

TEAM COMMUNICATION

In the previous dialogue, there certainly were moments when communication could have broken down completely. Both husband and wife created roadblocks to working out the problem together.

When you are trying to work as a team, I would like you to keep in mind two particularly important communication tips: *stick to the issue* and *avoid the middleman.* Let's examine what each suggestion entails.

1. Sticking to the Issue

Sometimes a simple discussion about a child's behavior can quickly escalate into a feud. For example:

Father: I don't like it when Lauren stays out late.

Mother: Neither do I!

Father: Can't you tell her to be home on time?

Mother: I do remind her! But you never say anything to her about it even when you are home, which isn't often!

Father: You know I have to work late a lot. What do you want from me?

Mother: A little support, that's all.

Father: You get support from me—my paycheck!

Mother: I don't want to feel that the raising of *our* children is *my* responsibility. I want your help, too.

Father: Every time we talk about the kids we end up fighting. This is ridiculous!

When discussion ensues over problems with children, the biggest energy drainer is speaking past the issue at hand. In the preceding example, the issue—Lauren's lateness—was forgotten and another issue—Father's lack of support for Mother—led to an argument. Energy is saved if we focus directly on the problem at hand and help our partner to do the same. When either party speaks past the issue, the discussion gets sidetracked. It takes that much longer to resolve the problem, if it is resolved at all.

The first step to take to help you and your partner keep to the issue is to recognize how each of you typically gets the communication off track. Some of the ways that adults sidetrack the discussion are:

- Taking offense at how your partner is talking to you ("How dare you talk to me in that tone of voice!")

- Bringing up other complaints ("I also don't like it when you . . . .")

- Challenging every argument that's presented ("How can you say that . . . ?")

- Giving excuses ("I had such a hard day at work.")

- Feeling hurt ("You don't care about how I feel.")

The next time you find yourself in a dispute, listen for some of these tactics that get the discussion off beam. When they occur, stop the discussion and insist, "Wait a minute! Let's figure out how we're going to solve the problem we have right now." This move freezes the action between you and allows you and your partner to refocus.

The second step to take to keep to the issue is to use some of the same techniques for staying calm and confident that were discussed in Chapter 4. Let's apply these techniques to Lauren's parents.

> Father: I don't like it when Lauren stays out late.
>
> Mother: Neither do I!
>
> Father: Can't you tell her to be home on time?
>
> Mother: I do remind her! But you never say anything to her about it even when you are home, which isn't often!
>
> Father: *You're right. I'm not home as much as I'd like to be. But right now, let's figure out what to do with Lauren.*
>
> Mother: Well, I tell her, but she doesn't seem to listen to me.
>
> Father: Would it help if we both talk to her?
>
> Mother: Yes, I think so. I don't want to feel that it's just my job.
>
> Father: You're right. Let's sit down with Lauren tonight. What exactly do we want to get across to her?

During the discussion, there were a few opportunities to get sidetracked. For instance, when Mother said, "But you never say anything about it when you are home, which isn't often," Father could have become angry and discussion might have become a fight, as in the first example. Talking directly, acknowledging the validity of the other person's remarks, and refocusing the discussion all help to avoid the escalation of a discussion into a battle.

2. Avoiding the Middleman

In our heart of hearts, most of us want our children to love us more than anyone else—maybe even more than our partner. This is a fairly natural reaction, but one that can cause problems for us, our spouse, and our children.

If you're angry with your spouse, you may vent your frustrations in the children's presence in such a way that you look good and your partner looks bad. Statements like "Your father's never here when I need him" or "It's fine with me if you go to the party" are usually said in anger. They have the effect, however, of pitting one parent against the other in children's eyes.

When there are conflicts between partners, it is important to talk with one another directly rather than through the children. Confronting your partner directly may feel less frightening if you believe you have the skills to do so effectively. When you communicate your reactions toward your partner in a descriptive, nonjudgmental way, the discussion is more likely to be productive. Saying to your partner, "You're just a pushover with the kids," is not easy for him to accept without becoming defensive and argumentative. It also conveys your dissatisfaction and anger but does not tell your partner exactly what behavior you are dissatisfied with. Discussion in Chapter 4 focused on clear, direct communications. In the same ways that these messages facilitate communication with children, they can help us say what we want to say to our partner—and be heard.

When you are the recipient of a negative general statement such as, "I don't like the way you deal with the children," you can also help yourself get more descriptive feedback by asking your partner to be more specific about the complaint. For example:

Father: I don't like the way you deal with the children.

Mother: What don't you like?

Father: Everything!

Mother: Something's really bothering you and I'd like to know what it is.

Father: Like tonight at dinner, Don didn't want to eat what we'd cooked so you made him something else.

Mother: You don't want me to make special orders for Don?

Father: No, he has to learn to eat different kinds of food, don't you think?

Mother: Sometimes I forget he's not a baby anymore. I think you're right. I shouldn't be doing that. Okay, what else do I do with the kids that bothers you?

Father: That's really all that was on my mind, I guess.

Mother: I'm glad we talked. I thought you were really
mad at me.

Of course, team communication between parents who are separated or divorced is often more difficult than between parents
who are together. Many single parents have hostile feelings toward
their ex-spouse and try, sometimes inadvertently, to turn the children away from their other parent. Children feel torn when their
parents say negative things about each other to them. The children
don't necessarily share these hostilities and usually want an ongoing
relationship with both parents. Efforts need to be made, therefore, to facilitate communication between the parents in order to
maintain a sense of stability for the children.

The same team communication skills discussed for two-parent
families will help to establish a consistent approach between
two parents who are separated or divorced. I recognize that time
to do this is limited by the fact that you're not in constant contact with each other. So it's important to negotiate times when
you will discuss your children, particularly those who are difficult, work out some of your differences of opinion about the
behaviors you want to promote, and develop consistent plans to
help the change occur.

PARENTS AND TEACHERS AS PARTNERS

Many team relationships affect your child's well-being, but other
than between parents the relationship between parents and
teachers ranks next in importance. All too often, however, the
relationship between the two parties is nonsupportive and even
antagonistic. Parents sometimes have little respect for their children's teachers, and teachers sometimes consider parents to be as
much of a nuisance as their children.

The rift between parents and teachers has become larger and
larger in recent times, and no simple solutions are available to
reduce it. For your part, however, I have ten suggestions.

1. Don't put down teachers in front of your child.

2. Understand that teachers are reluctant to admit they
   can't handle your child. Offer your help.

3. Tell teachers what you know about your child that may help them be successful.

4. Obtain specifics about classroom rules and the problems your child is having in school following them.

5. Offer to work out a joint plan for helping your child change her behavior in school. Utilize the ten basic options described in Chapter 5 as a framework for this planning.

6. In particular, suggest ways you can, at home, reward or penalize your child for behaviors engaged in at school. Ask if teachers would like to help in this way.

7. Consider a monitoring plan in which the school sends home frequent reports about your child's behavior. Write comments on the reports and have them returned to the school.

8. Send a note to the school principal praising teachers' teamwork with you.

9. In conferences with teachers, use confident communication techniques!

10. If you feel that there are strong conflicts between you and your child's teachers, assert your right to stand up for what you believe is in the best interests of your child. At the same time, work toward resolution of these conflicts, communicating cooperative intentions and understanding the teachers' perspective.

JOINING TOGETHER WITH OTHER PARENTS

Parents especially benefit from talking with other parents who have dealt with the same frustrations that accompany bringing up a child. Other parents share your frustrations and often have useful suggestions from their own experience. So, if you can, join a parent group, or start a group of your own where parents can come together and share their experiences and suggestions. Joining with other parents can be a tremendous source of support.

Questions and Answers

1. *I am divorced and my ex-spouse doesn't want anything to do with our child. Must I still try to include him?*

   Up to a point. The invitation should always be there. If he doesn't accept, so be it. But be as persistent as you reasonably can be. Your child will be the winner for it.

2. *I don't trust my husband's judgment and understanding of children. Isn't it better to be the parenting specialist in the family?*

   If you do, you are disqualifying him. It isn't easy sharing parenting but it's important.

3. *I depend on my mother to take care of my children for part of the day, but she's a very difficult person to team with. She's always critical of me and doesn't listen to my feelings. Any suggestions?*

   Yes. Try making a very small, specific request of her that she would find difficult to turn down (e.g., "I would like it if you would tell me something I do as a mother which you value. It would make me feel better"). Perhaps, not asking too much of her would make it possible to slowly build your relationship in a positive direction.

4. *What do I do if my child complains to me about her teacher and the complaint seems totally warranted?*

   This is a tricky situation because you don't want to reject your child's complaint, but you also don't want to undermine the teacher, who is, after all, a "teammate." I would assure your child that you will check out the complaint with the teacher and then deal privately with the teacher. Be careful not to express disrespect for the teacher to your child.

5. *What if two parents agree but their approach is harmful?*

   Of course, this creates a problem, but not as much as when the parents are in chronic conflict with each other. I'd rather see two parents jointly deciding to spoil a child than to constantly fight each other. Usually, parents who can agree with each other are capable of switching gears once they learn about the alternatives they have, such as the ten basic options.

7

A Short Review
of the Plan

In the Introduction, I promised a simple, four-step plan that is easy to remember and put into practice. I certainly hope that you will find this to be so.

After reading page after page of ideas and case examples, however, one can easily lose sight of the forest through the trees. To avoid this, I'd like to put the whole back together again by giving you a short review of the four-step plan. As I do this, keep in mind how each step applies to your situation.

STEP 1: GET CLEAR WHAT YOU WANT

What do you expect from your child?

Even though you may be concerned about your child's overall functioning, the only practical way to begin helping him is to examine where you stand with regard to your child's—

- Responsibilities
- Relationships
- Living habits
- Whereabouts
- Belongings

Take particular stock of the behaviors your child engages in that upset you and ask yourself how clear you are about what you want her to do instead.

Select one problem behavior that you would like to change. Ask yourself these questions:

- Do I really want to pursue a change in this behavior *at this time?*

- What specifically do I want to see changed?

- Are there any first steps my child can take to improve? Or do I want the entire situation improved?

- How much help, if any, am I willing to give my child to obtain the desired behavior?

- Do other adults have the same position as I?

When you are clear about your expectations, you can avoid the uncomfortable feeling that "you don't know what you're doing" in raising your child. *Remember that your position does not have to be strict or permanent to be clear.* It's also important to examine how you might confuse your child by your inconsistency or empty threats. Above all, realize that it is okay to experiment for a week with a particular position to see how it feels. Don't get frozen by indecisiveness.

STEP 2: REMAIN CALM AND CONFIDENT

How do you convey to your child what you want?

Even if it's difficult to communicate fully with your child, the way you come across will determine if you say what you mean and mean what you say. Generally speaking, staying calm and confident is far better than pleading or getting angry. Your quiet determination will win your child over sooner than begging or explosions ever will.

Remaining calm and confident is helped by STEP 1—getting clear what you want. Knowing where you are headed often gives you greater focus and control. Other suggestions to remain calm and confident include:

- Talk as little as warranted.

- Don't argue or justify everything.

- Slow down the pace of the battle.

- Don't get sidetracked.

- Catch yourself losing control and switch back to the issue.

If possible, try to check how your body language may be betraying your cause. Approach your child directly and establish good eye contact when making requests. Alter your voice to be slower, faster, louder, or softer than it normally is. Touch your child affectionately to gain cooperation and hold him firmly when restraining is appropriate. Accompany your directions or saying no with helpful gestures.

Remember that you show your real confidence by not being afraid to show interest in what your child has to say. You can listen, on occasion, to what she feels and should openly question, acknowledge, and empathize in response. You can also show your confidence in your child by inviting her cooperation as opposed to always ordering your child about.

STEP 3: SELECT A PLAN OF ACTION

What will help your child change his behavior in the direction you want?

Even if you have been clear about what you want and know how to sound and look as if you mean it, many problems still persist. When that is the case, the important thing to do is select one problem behavior as a place to begin helping your child. When children are difficult, parents have to make small inroads at first. Big change comes from small ones.

With one problem area as your focus, you must first identify the approaches you've taken that have been unsuccessful. Next, examine the menu of options you can use instead:

- Requesting

- Reminding

- Monitoring

- Ignoring

- Charting

- Rewarding

- Encouraging
- Teaching
- Backing Off
- Penalizing

As you consider and implement a new approach, remember to:

- Stick to your plan for one to two weeks to determine its effectiveness.
- Include other significant adults in your planning.
- Make sure the plan deals with changing a specific behavior. Be clear what you want.
- Inform your child about the plan where appropriate. Carry out the plan calmly and confidently.
- Avoid using the same option over and over again.

STEP 4: OBTAIN SUPPORT FROM OTHER ADULTS

Do I have support for the changes I am seeking?

Even though you may be determined to help your child change, you'll soon run out of gas or get blocked in traffic. The parenting of a child cannot easily be achieved by the efforts of one person alone. It takes a team.

A team approach involves a commitment to:

- Provide emotional support
- Give constructive feedback
- Plan together

In order to achieve sufficient levels of support, feedback, and planning, it is helpful to follow these guidelines:

- Set aside a special time to talk about your child.
- Request support for trying a new approach with your child.

- In small matters, be willing to be the disciplinarian by yourself.

- In large matters, check with your partner; don't take action by yourself.

- Allow your partner to handle the conflicts she gets into with your child.

- Resolve your differences in private.

As you communicate with all the important adults in your child's life (spouse, ex-spouse, teachers, etc.), remember to communicate clearly, directly, and with confidence. Show interest in what others have to say even when you disagree. Stick to the issue. Above all, work things out face-to-face. Avoid using your child as a middleman.

Before you go forth with the program, bear in mind the helpful beliefs contained in the first part of this book. *Your child can change!* Give him a chance to show you. Initially, you may see little to keep you optimistic. But then, again, Rome wasn't built in a day.

Remember also that your child needs you to be both involved and in charge. If you blend these jobs in the ways suggested by this book, your child will be the winner.

Index

About the Author

Mel Silberman, Ph.D., is Professor of Psychological Studies in Education at Temple University and is a family therapist in private practice.

He is coauthor of *How to Discipline Without Feeling Guilty* (Research Press) and the author of ten other books, as well as numerous journal articles, in the fields of education and psychology.

Since 1980, Dr. Silberman has lectured and given seminars to a wide range of parents and professionals. Sought after for his views on a variety of parenting concerns, he has been interviewed for magazine and newspaper articles throughout the country and has been invited to appear frequently on television and radio.

Do you conduct
parent training?

If you are a counselor, teacher, social worker, psychologist, minister, rabbi, nurse, or simply a concerned parent, you may wish to lead a parenting group based on the ideas contained in *When Your Child Is Difficult*.

Dr. Silberman's Confident Parenting Program is a fifteen-hour course loaded with skill-building activities to help parents master the ideas and techniques found in this book.

Dr. Silberman is also available to conduct programs and seminars for parent and professional organizations.

For further information concerning Confident Parenting Program materials and/or a program conducted by Dr. Silberman, contact:

Active Training
26 Linden Lane
Princeton, NJ 08540
telephone   (609) 924-8157
fax   (609) 924-4250
e-mail   mel@tigger.jvnc.net